What others are saying about
Positive x Positive = Unlimited . . .

"Thirty great ideas to get your life rocking! Tim G. Carter—a.k.a. 'Slam,' has written an insightful book filled with a practical, straight-to-the-point approach that works. He shares simple tips that anyone can benefit from. This book speaks directly to the heart and provides inspiration to help us lead a more authentic, purposeful, and happy life."

-Giovanni Gaudelli, Keynote and Motivational Speaker, Co-active Coach, Business Consultant and Sales Trainer

"Tim has written an excellent book that I think will help others greatly enhance their life and career. As Tim's pastor, I can certainly say he is one of the most positive individuals I have encountered. I have always wondered how Tim has been able to face every challenge and opportunity in life with such a positive attitude and to succeed in so many endeavors. In his new book, Tim shares the dynamic concepts that have not only given him such an amazing outlook on life, but have also fueled his success. This book requires some effort and discipline on the part of the reader, but anyone willing to interact with, reflect on, and apply these concepts to their life and career will quickly see both improve exponentially!"

-Cris Uren, Pastor, First United Methodist Church—
Thomasville, NC

*"To what do we liken Tim Carter?
How about a whirling dynamo of positive energy,
an innovator, a ball of fire, a joyful spirit? He is one
who always seeks a better way, a kinder way, a way
where everybody wins. Out of his faith and his
indomitable spirit, Tim inspires all who know him
and those who read his words to be better, kinder,
more efficient, and to do so with joy and enthusiasm
for work and for life itself."*

-Ed Lewis, Attorney—Thomasville, NC.

"Timothy Grant Carter simply HAD to write a book on how the exponential effects of being positive in life can make us unlimited! You see, 'positive' and 'unlimited' are at the core of Tim's nature! He also HAD to do it in a way that sets the reader up for DAILY success, because again, his very nature drives and compels him to make every day great! This book is a SLAM DUNK if you want a day-by-day blueprint for taking life by the heart and making yours great! If you desire a life that's significant, SLAM is the man to take you there! If you want to have greater influence and impact, hold on to your bootstraps—SLAM delivers!"

*-Margo DeGange, M.Ed., Best-Selling Author, Speaker,
Publisher, and Founder of Women of Splendor*

POSITIVE^2 = UNLIMITED
(positive x positive = unlimited)

Also by Splendor Publishing

The Art & Science of Loving Yourself First
'cause Your Business Should Complete You Not Deplete You!

25 Brilliant Business Mentors
Their Top Tips to Catapult You to Success

The Happy Law Practice
Expert Strategies to Build Business
While Maintaining Peace of Mind

The Influential Entrepreneur
Position Yourself for Win-Win Engagement

Winning Ways in Commercial Real Estate
18 Successful Women Unveil the Tips of the Trade
in the Real Estate World

Accessorizing for Design Professionals
A Guide for Interior Designers,
Decorators, and Color Consultants

The Substance of Faith
Get Hooked—It's Good Stuff!

POSITIVE^2 = UNLIMITED

(positive x positive = unlimited)

*H*igh

*O*ctane

*P*ositive

*E*nergy

Thirty Readings of Inspirational Thoughts to Add Meaning to Your Life and Career!

Timothy Grant Carter

Splendor Publishing
College Station, TX

SPLENDOR PUBLISHING
Published by Splendor Publishing
College Station, TX.

First published printing, November, 2014

Library of Congress Control Number: 2014954742
Positive x Positive = Unlimited: High Octane Positive Energy
1. Business 2. Self Help

ISBN-10:1940278198
ISBN-13:978-1-940278-19-3
Business/Self Help

Printed in the United States of America.

Cover Background: © Diabluses | Dreamstime.com

For more information or to order bulk copies of this book for events,
seminars, conferences, or training, please contact

SplendorPublishing.com

Dedication

My sister, Detra Carol Carter, was my closest friend.
She made statements that have molded my thinking. Her
artwork revolutionized my creativity. Her encouragement
kept me going in times when I would have otherwise quit.
Her sharing kept my heart open and my mind sharp.
I dedicate this book to her. She would be overjoyed to see it
and without her it would not exist. I miss her greatly.

Contents

FOREWORD

by Steve Gutzler

Tim Carter's desire to help people discover their purpose and develop their God-given potential is apparent in everything he does, and this dynamic book is no exception. Over the last three decades since we first met in a small college in Los Angeles, Tim has remained the same friend and inspiring leader. We have spent many hours sharing our hopes for our families, vision for our businesses, and goals in life. It is obvious to me Tim is a great person and a great leader, and as you read the pages of this book, I know you will also benefit from his positive and inspiring insights.

Tim's words empower you. No matter the pain of your past or the problems in your present, Tim will compel you to maximize your potential in life. If you desire to write your own chapters that include health, happiness, and fulfillment, this book can take you to the next level. Regardless of your current circumstances, get ready for a great dose of hope and empowerment.

Tim's book is a must read. But I encourage you to do more than just read this book . . . Commit to live it!

Steve Gutzler
President, Leadership Quest
Issaquah, WA

SteveGutzler.com
MyVisionCoach.com

INTRODUCTION

Why would you want to read a book from a guy known as "**Slam**"? Because that nickname was given to me for my reputation of being a power-house! I resurrected the nickname a few years ago, because it says something about what I want to give to others in the marketplace. *Dynamism*! I want to share with you dynamic concepts that will enhance your life and career. That is the underlying vision behind this book.

A previous business partner gave the concepts I teach a nickname. She called my thinking "Slam-ism." So hang on and I will share a healthy dose of it with you. In these pages, let's learn together to dynamically improve our lives and careers.

Several years have passed since I first decided to write this book. Writing is not a new task for me. It has been a life-long passion. In younger years, I developed and wrote a previous book—which was three times longer than this one. Yet, it wasn't what I wanted to publish as my first solo book, so it was shelved. It remains unpublished. Who knows, I may come back to it. But I have moved on in my writing interests. In the last three years, I have written over 275 articles, and more than 2,000 sales tips, and co-authored another published book *(25 Brilliant Business Mentors: Their Top Tips to Catapult You to Success)*.

I resolved that my first published solo book had to be very useful to large numbers of people. With this in mind, the subject matter of this book was born, from proven marketplace usefulness.

Eight years ago, I started a career selling manufactured and modular housing. That workplace gave me the opportunity to present ideas at store and regional meetings, which helped and inspired co-workers. In the process of developing and presenting these concepts to assist colleagues in the workplace, I watched with satisfaction as the ideas did magic for them. I realized I had found the substance for a book—a solid resource everyone needs: power tools showing how to enjoy our careers and get more gratification and satisfaction from them. Nearly everyone is interested in improving their performance in the part of their lives that consumes most of their waking hours.

The colleagues I initially presented these concepts to, enjoyed the benefits of them, and it was their comments that led me to the commitment to turn these ideas into a book. I saw that if these lessons gave them greater hope, then many others could be strengthened from them as well.

We all *hope* we can achieve more. We *hope* we can find greater fulfillment in our work, and most of us *hope* we can improve our performance. So from this idea, part of the title (the subtitle, actually) of this book was born. **HOPE** . . .

High **O**ctane **P**ositive Energy

Still, it seemed that the title needed more. Beyond HOPE, I was looking for a phrase that really summed up the essence of what I wanted to teach in the book. A friend—Richard—who I helped in many dimensions of his life (and who has since passed away), provided the thought I needed. After describing the idea of this book to him, he exclaimed, *"That's it! What you are trying to say, Tim, is positive times positive equals unlimited!"* BINGO! I knew *that* was it. I knew Richard had nailed what I wanted to say in this book . . .

Positive² (Positive x Positive) = Unlimited!

I knew that the *multiplied effects* of applying the principles given here would do more than just add to people's lives and happiness. I understood if people would really apply these truths and techniques on top of each other, they would not only gain additional success, but *multiply* additional success.

So my commitment to write this book became strong, because I knew it could make a difference in many lives. But this book is like gas in the pump at the filling station: it will give you no power, until you put it in your tank. These lessons must be worked on *daily*, for a period of time, if they are to have the best possible effect on your profession and life overall.

I wrote this book in the same way I developed it: in doses. Good medicine often only benefits you if you take it on a regular basis. So I designed the doses of the medicine to come to you in thirty readings. You must be disciplined enough to read one each day. You must be dedicated to get out a clean notebook and work on each reading's content, with your own ideas of personal application.

Why? You can taste the water but it does you no good till you drink it in. Likewise, the cleansing, elevating properties of this book will do you no good unless you jump in, and personally apply them. You are going to have to "work" at it, so you can find the deepest treasure within these pages. Yet that is the message of this book . . . work is good. Work is necessary—and it can even be fun!

Practicing positive directions can add tremendously to your life. Practicing positive empowerments in multiple areas simultaneously creates a living *explosion* of growth. The thoughts in this book can be *exponentially empowering* (hence, **Positive²**). I remind you of this throughout the text by calling each awesome possibility an "***Exponential Idea***."

Each morning the birds sing anew. Each day nature brings new joys of life. So nature teaches us that life is a daily thing. The Great Master Jesus told us to approach life asking for our daily bread. He also told us not to fret about tomorrow but only be concerned with the things we can change today. The serenity prayer keeps us in the peace of accepting what we cannot change. I can only change today. I *can* change today. I *must* change today to achieve the maximum possible productivity and happiness in my life. So with God's help, let's make today great.

Each daily ***Exponential Idea*** is designed so you can take each day afresh, as denoted by the little logo, "*Make Today Great.*" Start reading right away. Don't put it off. First, get a blank notebook and a pen. You will need them for maximum benefit. I want you to win, and for that to happen, you must know that it is not my ideas, but the *development of your own ideas* that will cause you to really grow, develop and achieve.

So Slam says, "*Let's go to work! Let's add **Positive²** to our professional and personal lives!*"

I have one important note to you free spirits! If you're having a blast reading the book, go ahead! You can come back through for the daily application after you have enjoyed reading the book! Go for it!

Dive in!

Tim G. Carter—a.k.a. "Slam"

MAKE TODAY GREAT

4

MAKE TODAY GREAT

EXPONENTIAL IDEA 1

Positive X Positive = Unlimited

Key Idea

Positive Influence Changes vs. Positive Dimension Shifts

Adding more consistent positive influences to your life can multiply your results. The word "positive" is so overworked, that its power is at times overlooked.

Adding positive influences to your situation obviously will improve your effectiveness. This is plain. What is not so obvious is that adding positive dimensions to your life can not only improve your results, but literally "multiply" your outcome. This can radically change your life for the good!

❧❧

What is a positive dimension? It is not just a one-time occurrence, but a consistent addition to your life.

Here are some examples of positive dimensions vs. positive influences. Adding a positive dimension is not just listening to a different song, but changing the channel. It is not just having a different thought but learning a different way of thinking. It is not just meeting a new acquaintance but entirely changing the way you view and engage in relationships. It is not just adding an activity to your life but adopting an entirely more active lifestyle.

When you improve major dimensions of your life, your whole life can change for the good. These dimensions can become more than influences that add value to each other. They can snowball into something much greater. When you add whole dimensions of good to your life, these positive forces (dimensions) multiply themselves times themselves to create more value and worth. I think this is what Steven Covey meant by the term *"paradigm shift."*

A deep, heart-felt paradigm shift can involve changes in several positive dimensions. Conversely, a meaningful change in several key dimensions can result in a major paradigm shift of your life. The point is that positively changing significant dimensions of your life can greatly enhance your path and productivity.

What are some dimensions you can improve to radically change the effectiveness of your life and career? Perhaps your private thought life, relationships, recreational pursuits, health habits, spiritual discipline, and mental outlook, to name a few.

You need to name your own for this to really work. While it is true that changing activities can add to your effectiveness, improving whole dimensions can totally transform your potential.

Here is a personal example of what I mean. When I was much younger, I had associates who pulled me down. Every time I associated with them, character traits that were not healthy would occur. To deal with this, I disassociated from friends I decided were not a good influence. I not only changed what I did with the friends, I changed the friends!

The positive result of this decision led me to transform the whole dimension of my relationships. I developed the practice of evaluating every association on the basis of whether it is healthy and constructive. I've now seen the multiplied results of many years of choosing to personally associate with those who are a positive asset to my life. The adage goes, "*You don't get to choose your family, but you do choose your friends.*"

I am not too proud to receive help from others. I am not too uncaring to give help to others. But the overall direction of the relationship must be good, or I will sever or limit the tie. Likewise, if the relationship is good for me and my friend, I will strengthen the bonds. By making this sweeping change in the area of my relationships, I have radically changed my life for the good.

There are many areas where you can not only change certain aspects of your life, but whole dimensions. You will find that such major positive life shifts will powerfully change your life for the good. Positive x positive = unlimited.

❧☙

Action Required

Develop a strategy of major positive changes to improve important dimensions of my life. Use this book as a catalyst to start.

Phrase to Memorize

"*I can radically change my life and career for the good.*"

MAKE TODAY GREAT

EXPONENTIAL IDEA 2

Worth is Believing in Your Own Value

Key Idea

Developing a Sense of Worth is a Critical Component in a Healthy Life

To be fully human demands that we achieve a deep self-realization. Self-realization begins with knowing who we are. So, if our quest to be in touch with ourselves is to be a healthy journey, it must begin with a knowledge of self-worth and personal value.

⋙⋘

A figure called Polonius in Shakespeare's famous play Hamlet, said some of the most powerful words in human history: *"To thine own self be true."* Though these famous words come from a drama of fiction, scarcely any words can be truer to life.

If we do not believe in our own value, we can never achieve our full potential. We cannot contribute to others until we realize our own significance. During pre-flight instructions, flight attendants advise parents in case of a loss of cabin pressure to first put on their own oxygen mask. Why would a parent put themselves before their child? Because if the parent is not conscious and self-aware, they cannot care for and sustain their dependent. It is clearly true that taking care of ourselves is a huge part of being able to do anything for others.

No one can pour from an empty cup. If we do not find value in our existence, then we cannot give to others. To contribute, we must first believe in our own worth.

It drives me crazy when I listen to sales representatives, and their only well-made point is what the competition does or does not do. While it is true we need to be marketplace savvy, and in the workplace we must know what our competition is doing, our personal excellence will only grow when we focus on the awesomeness of our own brand and service. Believe in your own value. Sell your own value.

When someone ridicules you in the workplace and doubts your ability, *sell your own value*. When someone in your home-life does not believe in you, and discourages you instead of supporting and encouraging you, *sell your own value*.

By selling your own value, you can pull yourself out of nearly any situation. Ascribing your own value is not pride, ego, or hedonism. It is acknowledging the worth your creator has deposited in your being. It is a necessary mindset to grow towards the threshold of higher realms of potential in life.

For truly, it is impossible to please our Divine Master if we do not multiply the gifts He has given us. The stewardship of maximizing our talents is clearly a scriptural mandate (Matt. 25:14-30). Please read this "Parable of the Talents" for one of the clearest stories on how important the correct use of our abilities is to God. Therefore, from even the most reverent point of view, it is imperative that we learn to *sell our own value.*

With a true sense of self-worth we also affirm the value of those around us, and consequently, acknowledging the merit of others actually increases our capacity for self-worth. If a glass is clean we can see through both ways! In the same way, a healthy outlook can also lead to a more meaningful in-look.

Part of realizing our worth is in understanding our own significance. To have a happier life, we must credit ourselves for the worthwhile things we do. We should pay attention to the score cards of others; they can be very revealing. Additionally, we should keep our own score card. Then, if no one else praises us, we can at least give ourselves proper credit for the good we do. We should stay off our own back! The song, "Don't Worry. Be Happy," is over simplistic, but many times I have found that it is good advice. Self-esteem is built on a frame of solid self-worth.

The Energizer Bunny keeps going and going because of good batteries. We also need a good internal power source if we are to sustain meaningful efforts in our own life. A healthy sense of worth is a great internal power source. It also can keep us going and going. It is a great energizer.

One thing that prevents many from learning this power source, is confusing a good sense of self-worth with being *self—ish.* Worth is neither pride nor egotism. Worth honestly appraises our own performance while still realizing the need for developmental growth. Worth credits God and others for indispensable importance, while still realizing its own value. Worth grows in proper context to the value of others. It finds meaning in reality and courtesy, and even in humility. Worth grows a healthy self-concept that respects this same need in others.

Still, if we must believe in ourselves to advance in the pursuit of personal growth. The question is then, how do we grow to feel better about ourselves? The answer starts in how we talk to ourselves *about* ourselves.

To grow personally, our self-talk must be healthy. We must develop our own self-worth beliefs and statements, and say them about ourselves. We must learn to have an internal dialogue that says and believes positive things about ourselves. This habit can completely change the way we feel and behave. This will cause us to have a healthier self-worth; and a healthy self-worth will keep us working harder, smarter, and with more satisfaction—on any career path.

❧❧

Action Required

Develop and write down positive statements of worth, and say them daily.

Phrases to Memorize

1. *"I will believe in my own worth and value, and be happier and healthier."*

2. *"My Personal excellence will grow, and I will focus on the awesomeness of my own brand and service."*

3. *"I will grow to feel better about myself, by thinking about how I talk to myself, about myself."*

MAKE TODAY GREAT

EXPONENTIAL IDEA 3

Resolve: Get in the Wheelbarrow

Key Idea

Investing All of Your Capacity Towards a Worthy Goal is Sometimes the Only Way to Win

୶ৡৡ৶

One day, I marched into our morning meeting at work with a paper bag and a request to explain. When asked to speak, I pulled a red aerosol can from the bag containing Resolve carpet spot remover.

The can worked. It got people's attention and caused them to think. The can's contents promised to remove stains instantly and to be deeply penetrating. Many challenges in our life require an instant answer. To postpone it will not do, and to delay it will mean defeat. Therefore, we need instant *resolve*.

Many obstacles also require more than just a surface answer. They require that our focus be deeply thought through and worked out in a truly penetrating way.

Resolve is this kind of quality. It can take immediate effect and still have deep, far reaching implications. Resolve is the catalyst that turns gas into RPMs. Resolve is the power that turns theory into practice; to thoroughly resolve a decision in your mind takes it from indecision to a solid course of action.

I love old boxing movies. In true Rocky style, most of them show a boxer beaten into his corner, who, upon some inspiration, emerges as a completely new fighter. The man who was clearly beaten only moments before is now unbeatable. The disheartened man now comes forth as the champion with valor.

This is the kind of thing resolve will do. It can take your negative thoughts and turn them into positive action. It can take your indecision and turn it into courageous performance.

Which area of your life needs the dynamic force of resolve? Ask yourself what it is you know to do, and only fail at because of a lack of commitment. This is the life stain that needs resolve.

The tale is told of a great tightrope walker who had a friend who promised his unwavering belief in him. When the famous high wire artist announced he was going to walk a wire with a wheelbarrow across Niagara Falls, his friend pledged a great sum to show his belief that his friend could accomplish the feat. So on the day of the event, the tightrope walker decided to test his friend's commitment. When he was ready to start the task, he told his friend, *"If you really believe in me, hop into the wheelbarrow."* Suddenly his friend realized the limits to his conviction. Still, this brings us back to what we really mean by *resolve.*

Resolve hops in the wheelbarrow (my crazy cat, Nietzsche, has the idea)! Resolve doesn't talk about commitment; it walks it through! Resolve dedicates itself to achieve the objective and stays focused on the task, regardless of the price tag.

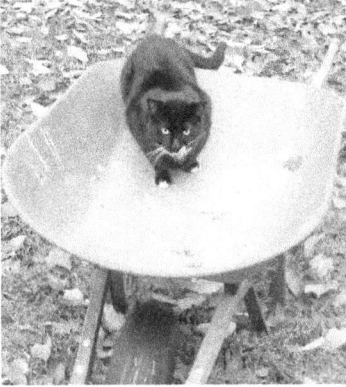

Maybe the life solution you need is firmer resolution. Let's think about that again . . . maybe . . . the life solution you need is firmer resolution.

How could your life and career benefit from a deeper resolution? Could a firmer resolve be the fuel you are looking for, to improve your performance?

❦

Action Required

Identify the area(s) that need your commitment, and resolve yourself to the solution.

Phrase to Memorize

"I can resolve to change my indecision into courageous performance."

EXPONENTIAL IDEA 4

Interest: Turn it Upside Down

Key Idea

Often the Solution We Seek is Only a Different Perspective

Many times in adversity, people need to be reminded, *"You can't see the forest for the trees."* It is common for people to be so wrapped up in their personal circumstance, they cannot see objectively. Our answer is often right in front of us, if we could only see from a different point of view.

❧❧

Often, we have problems that look like unmanageable giants: giants that can be scaled down to size when we take a different point of view. The limitation stopping you may not be the circumstance itself. The thing holding you back may just be the way you are looking at it! It could be that looking at the

17

situation differently might hold the key to unlocking your answer.

I love to observe babies as they watch the world around them: no preformed opinions, no predetermined ideas—just brand new fresh eyes experiencing their surroundings for the first time.

Sometimes we need the lack of prejudice and bias that a baby possesses, to be able to look at a situation from a completely new view point. We need this objectivity to truly see what is going on around us. When a baby studies his or her world, it is not as a casual observer. No . . . a baby watches things with fascination (like my grandson Jaxson, pictured here). A baby marvels at the things we take for granted; everything is interesting to a small child. The simplest things—the feel of a blanket, the song of a bird, or the dance of a butterfly—completely captivate a child's senses. Yet adults barely acknowledge them when such wonders occur.

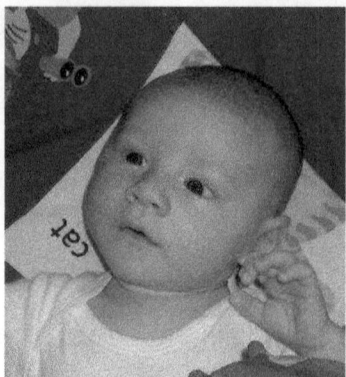

We would be well served to awaken our fascination with simple things. Sometimes simply having more interest in our surroundings can produce the vision we need. Often the answer only escapes us because we have not looked more intently into the commonplace around us. Frequently, we can discover that the present moment is more magical than mundane: if we will only look at our roadblocks with more childlike fascination and curiosity.

I had a good friend who was also the president of a company in which I worked for many years. His name was Wolfgang Hafele. He was one of the greatest teachers I ever had in life.

Wolfgang had an uncanny problem-solving ability. He could look at a situation with a completely fresh perspective. He could see things by throwing out all the "givens," and by passing up on all the *"This is the way it has been done before"* syndromes, he could turn a situation upside down. Wolfgang could change the oil on his own thinking, eliminating the old and replacing it with new. He was a truly brilliant man.

He was not afraid to try something new, and thus he taught me the value of unconventional approaches. Even when it had always been done a certain way before, his thinking allowed him to look at things as if he was seeing them for the first time. Wolfgang Hafele was therefore able to combine the innovation of a fresh approach with the great reservoirs of his wisdom and experience.

Life and careers should not be static experiences; they should be vital and growing. Learning should not be just a school-age experience, but a lifelong mission. Keeping a sense of mystery and wonder will enliven your career and enrich your life.

❧❧

Action Required

Try a new angle on your current challenges. It could be just the problem solver you need.

Phrase to Memorize

"My answer may be right in front of me, if I can only see from a different point of view."

MAKE TODAY GREAT

EXPONENTIAL IDEA 5

Ideal Image: Personal Competence

Key Idea

If You Don't Believe in Yourself, No One Else Will Either

⋘⋙

One morning while listening to AM talk radio, I heard an ad promoting a company called "Ideal Image." I was struck with the thought of the company's title. It depicts a condition that everyone wants to present to others.

Frequently, we miss conveying our ideal image to others, due to an inadequate belief in ourselves. We cannot show an impressive persona if we do not first have real confidence in our own ability. To show others our value, we must see our own potential for competent performance.

In order to picture an "ideal image" to others, you must first have a clear idea of your own inner uniqueness and attractive identity. You cannot communicate to others what you do not believe to be true about yourself.

So, if we do not possess such an internal "ideal image," how do we develop one? A good beginning is to make a list of your own positive, personal inventory.

If you want to improve your image at work, make a job-relevant asset list. What abilities do you possess that could help you in your career? Write these down for several days, until reading the list makes you feel better about yourself. Then daily, go over this list, while you define and refine what you believe to be good about your own performance capacity.

My background as a public speaker has provided practical means to take these new convictions and relate them to others. Literally, practice in front of the mirror, sharing your abilities to the image looking back at you. If you can become believable to yourself, then you will be much more prepared to discuss your talents to clients, work associates, and superiors.

Learning to relate your own abilities and potential is not egotistical . . . far from it! Being able to share your own strengths with conviction will assure your superiors and relax your customers. They will feel more assured about your skill in handling their needs and requests. Talking to someone who is uneasy about their own ability can be very discomforting. Conversely, talking to someone who clearly knows what they can do is very encouraging and reassuring.

By learning to believe in and share your abilities, you can develop a more "ideal image." In fact, this practice can turn your shortages into strengths. The story is told of Demosthenes, the greatest orator in ancient history. It is related that he overcame a major speech impediment by practicing speaking with stones in his mouth. Into the wind at the sea, he would practice until he could overcome stones and wind, both with his voice clarity. In this way, he not only overcame his impairment, but turned the area of his greatest deficiency into his greatest strength.

One great truism my brother, John, taught me about selling is, *"Never introduce a negative."* This is particularly true in selling, but also very pertinent in many aspects of business life. Deal with negatives when they occur but do not be the one to bring them up. Be known as a person who solves problems more than a person who seems to be identified by them.

Finally, but importantly in developing an ideal image, learn to handle rejection. My friend Cecil Stanley taught me a saying that helps a salesman have a progressive attitude: *"Some will, some won't, so what!"* Don't let the "No" bog you down. Stay light, stay loose, stay focused on your goals.

❧

Action Required

I will learn to present a more ideal image.

Phrase to Memorize

"If I believe, then I can achieve."

MAKE TODAY GREAT

EXPONENTIAL IDEA 6

Three Ss:The Value of a Fulfilling Purpose

Key Idea

***To Feel Good About What We Do, We Must Have a Good
Reason Why We Do It***

❧

Purpose is like an internal power drive. When we have it, we can keep on where others have stopped, and succeed where others have failed. The activities we do daily are more meaningful when they are part of something we believe deeply and consistently.

To get a clearer idea about the value of a fulfilling purpose, let's think about three words that begin with S: *singleness*, *satisfaction*, and *star*.

The first word, *singleness*, is a seldom used term that means commitment to a primary purpose with a singular focus. A robin works fervently because it believes in the importance of the nest it is constructing. Have you ever seen a depressed robin? No! Nature has instilled in these wonderful creatures a sense of the worth of their being. One twig at a time, one tiny piece at a time, a robin will continue relentlessly until its work is done and its nest is fashioned with care. Likewise, in our work, we need a course that compels us. We need a reason for doing our tasks that will keep us on course, even when facing difficulty and challenges. What is your cause for work? Focusing on this primary reason can keep you singularly motivated to do a good job, when all other hype and rhetoric fails.

The second "S" word that can help us experience the value of a fulfilling purpose is *satisfaction*. Sometimes the scope of our work can seem menial or insignificant, unless we feel satisfaction in contributing to a larger picture. When the leaf thinks its own role is unimportant, it can gain satisfaction in thinking about the larger role of the tree. If that is not enough, the leaf can derive satisfaction from the part it plays in the greatness of the forest. What is it about the location, service, or scope of the company you work for, that can cause you to feel satisfied in the good of what you do? Learning to find real satisfaction in the function of what you do can lead you to enjoy your work.

The third "S" word that can cause us to find deeper purpose in our vocational lives is *star*. A star may be part of the sky, but it shines with its own individual light. It is good to feel a part of something grander. But it is also good to feel you are a grand part of the larger design.

Consider the rose. It is certainly single in being what it is designed to be. It is certainly satisfied in its function and purpose. More importantly, the rose does all of this while expressing its individual radiance. Being excellent or beautiful in what you can do can produce its own rewards.

You can shine in the workplace without being egotistical. In fact, when you contribute a stellar performance in your own place in the workforce, you will add value to your company or organization. This is service, not selfishness.

Dave Akers, while a Regional Manager with Palm Harbor Homes, gave me some advice I will never forget. *"Never sacrifice what you are good at for anybody."*

Be singly focused on your own job like a robin building its nest. Be satisfied with what you do, because you know why you do it. Be like the rose. Stand out in striking attraction, in your own place of performance.

❧❧

Action Required

Realize the *why*, behind the *what* you do, to feel good about doing it.

Phrase to Memorize

Don't forget to star in your job performance. It will build your company or organization and add fulfillment and rewards to your own life and career.

MAKE TODAY GREAT

EXPONENTIAL IDEA 7

The Promise of Potential

Key Idea

Potential is the Promise that We Can Achieve Accomplishments in Life of Epic Proportions

❧❧

Think about the difference in the value of things that have fulfilled potential and things that have not. Consider a paper quarter wrapper. It reads ten dollars all over its design. It is made for the express purpose to hold ten dollars. But without the contents—which it is designed to hold—it is just an empty, flat piece of paper.

Yet when you fill the wrapper with forty quarters, it becomes valuable . . . it is worth its potential. The same wrapper, different value. Similarly, so are our lives. We may be designed to hold certain kinds of fulfillment. We may have the ability to achieve greatness, but until we fulfill the empty areas of our potential, we are like the wrapper. We are flat, empty, and of minimal value.

So how do we take the untapped potential of our lives and realize the promise of maximized possibilities? One solid way to look at these prospects is in the same way we would look at fulfilling the value of an empty quarter pack. By saving, giving, and growing, we can turn empty, worthless wrappers into things of value and merit.

Oh how I wish I had paid more attention to the concept of compound interest when I was much younger. If you diligently save, a little can become a lot! A little on a regular basis adds up, when saved consistently. Then you add interest to the savings and compound the interest with the principle and accumulate more.

The two keys of being able to successfully save to achieve potential are to "start now" and "be consistent." Many mean to save but never get around to it (one round tuit). Now you have a round tuit. So start immediately.

Seriously, in order to fulfill potential, you must get started right away. The quarter wrapper will never have forty quarters until you first put one in the pack. And then the one will never turn into forty unless you consistently keep adding quarters. So the message is to save; start now and keep saving.

The second really important part of achieving potential is giving. This is an ironic part of fulfillment. How can you become more, by giving away what you have? It is comparable to a spring. If you stop the flow, it becomes stagnant and lifeless, and eventually dries up. Yet if you keep the spring clean and allow the free flow of water from its ongoing source, the water it produces is purer and more plentiful. We have a benevolent progenitor, who assures that the sources of our life and well-being are deep, reliable, and inexhaustible—as long as we don't plug up the flow. And the surest way to keep the spring clean and make sure its life giving resource is free flowing, is by sharing it with others.

How can giving to others increase our own value? I remember when I was a young adult and wrapped up in my own problems. My mother talked me into going with her as a Yokefellow counselor, to talk to inmates at a local prison. The results were amazing! Somehow, by getting my mind on helping those incarcerated men, my problems seemed lighter; by giving, I found out I had more to give.

In the workplace, you may have a colleague who is struggling. You may be surprised at the results if you lend a hand. Not only may you help a fellow worker do a better job, you are likely to feel better about your own job performance and value. On top of saving, try giving as a way to achieve more of your potential. There are empty places in others' lives only you can fulfill.

Ultimately, in order to achieve more in our lives, we must grow! Growth is exploring new ground. Growth is trying new things. Growth is finding a way to increase and improve your performance. Find an area of need—like an empty quarter pack—and begin to invest in filling that vacant part of your life. How? Explore new ways to use a dormant talent! Employ creative strategies to invest and improve lacking relationships! Try methods to learn or start different avenues of improving your work performance.

Contentment is great when it is satisfaction over a fulfilled potential; contentment is complacent when it overlooks ways we can save, give, and grow to become happier, more fulfilled persons.

৵৽

Action Required

Identify and invest in three different areas of unfulfilled potential. Write down these areas of need. Then write down how you are going to try to save, give, and grow in the areas you have identified.

Phrase to Memorize

"By saving, giving, and growing, I can achieve accomplishments of epic proportions."

MAKE TODAY GREAT

EXPONENTIAL IDEA 8

Determination (Play on Words)

DETERMINATION

Daily
Energetic
Tenacious
Empowerment
Ready Mind/Relentless
Motivated
Inner Fortitude
Necessary
Action
Trainable
Inspired/Imaginative
On Task
New/Now!

Key Idea

Determination Should Transform Daily Personal Efforts into the Steps of Success

❧❧

The acrostic on the previous page is designed for you to hang on your office wall. Think about it on a daily basis and use it as a catalyst to become more determined in your work performance. The need for determination is so obvious, it's easy to overlook it and not focus on applying it.

Determination cannot be on again and off again for it to work. If Lance Armstrong had tried one day and not the next, he never would have achieved all of his Tour De France victories (regardless of the controversies that have happened since). He had to have daily determination. Determination cannot be half-hearted. It must be focused with good energy and tenacious application.

Determination will not help you win from the sidelines. You must be willing to get in the game and be empowered in the real task. If you are not ready to try your best now—and with relentless pursuit—determination will not help you overcome. Though the attainment of your goals may seem far away, you must be motivated *during* the task, just like you were at the start and like you will be at the finish line.

Many fall short in their determination because opposition or challenge wets the fire of their effort. It takes inner fortitude to find the fruits of true determination.

Also, determination is a step many would like to skip. However, it might not be easy to skip. Determination is not avoidable if you are to win in the workplace and in life.

Determination is not just needed by some, but by all. Determination is necessary for anyone who wants to succeed.

It is easy to get all worked up and "feel determined," but feelings will not translate into accomplishment unless they are accompanied by action. Determination is more than just a feeling.

Furthermore, determination should not be confused with bullheadedness. Determination is not naivety. In our determination, we must be a student of the game and open to new approaches. It has been well said (by Albert Einstein) that *"insanity is trying the same thing over and over and expecting different results."* So we must be trainable in our determination, to expect success. We need to be inspired enough to try alternative methods, and imaginative enough to try new approaches in our focused determination. This must become a reality if we want to experience the fruit of determination, which is *success.*

Finally, those who are really applied and determined in their pursuits, seem also to be those who most easily overcommit. You cannot do everything at once. To achieve something, you can't be wrapped up in everything! To win at important tasks, you will need to prioritize the energy of your determination and focus on the most essential ones. Plainly, true determination is moderated by realism and intelligence.

Most importantly, if you're going to win, your determination cannot get old. You must commit every day, and not wait until tomorrow to start. If your determination is going to help you succeed, then the mission to win must start fresh every day. It is like any good runner knows: you do not run to the finish line but past the finish line to win the race and achieve your best.

❧❧

Action Required

Decide on one or two tasks on which to double down the wager of your determination. Identify how this new focus will change your actions in these areas.

Phrase to Memorize

Feelings will not translate into accomplishments unless they are accompanied by action.

MAKE TODAY GREAT

EXPONENTIAL IDEA 9

Sales (Play on Words)

Key Idea

Everyone is a Salesman

Life is all about sales. You cannot win in the game of life without your own brand and style of salesmanship.

❦

Selling is not just a career; it is a necessity of life. You cannot successfully exist without selling along the way, no matter who you are!

Think about it. When a child really wants something, they try to sell their parents on why they should have it. A teenager does a selling job to get their license and very often, to get their first car. If you have ever had a close relationship, you did a selling job to win your companion. Every employment situation you have ever engaged in required that you first sell your talents, ability, and potential to your employer. The list of circumstances in your life that require you to sell to survive and thrive, goes on and on. So sharpening the skills of presenting yourself positively is good for everyone. Improving the ability to convince and persuade others will not only help a salesman, it will help you!

The acrostic below is designed to do just that: help you assess and grow in the area of salesmanship.

SALES (Play on Words)

Sharpness
Attitude
Listening
Education
Solutions

SALES—The first "S" is for *sharpness*. Every salesman knows that first impressions are not only important, but critical. People will not buy from you if they do not like you or think you do not know what you are doing. You must be sharp to win friends and influence people.

Think how much of your daily life could improve by being sharper. If you take your mate for granted and do not occasionally try to dress sharply for them, they will feel neglected and your relationship will suffer. If you do not try to do your best to be your best, it negatively affects every area of your life. Practice being sharp, and watch how much it benefits you.

SALES—"A" is for *attitude*. You can have a correct viewpoint but a poor attitude and people will not believe you. If you want a more favorable experience and treatment from those around you, try looking at your relationships differently. Try to think of, and adopt, a more positive approach. It is amazing what a difference you can make by simply approaching the situation with a smile. A healthy outlook and a good attitude can help you improve nearly every facet of your life and career.

SALES— "L" is for *listening*. Sometimes we do not "hear" people when we hear them. Their meaning flies right by us, because we were not focusing on what they said. Mike Moquin, a corporate vice president in my last position, spent quite some time teaching me how to actively listen. Learn to ask questions about what people are telling you. Do not feign interest, but drop what you are doing and genuinely try to understand not only *what*, but *why* people are speaking to you. Repeat what they say in your own words, to see if you got it right and if you really understand them. Learning to more deeply and sincerely listen can improve your spiritual, social, and career experience. Try listening better and hearing more.

SALES—"E" is for *education*. No matter how sincere you are, no one likes stupidity. Be a student of the important areas of your life. Read about relationships. Read about health. Read about your career. Work on becoming more knowledgeable and informed in the key areas of your life. Education should not just be a task for school, but a passion we pursue far beyond the classroom.

SALES—The last "S" is for *solution*. As previously mentioned, it has been well said (by Albert Einstein) that *"Insanity is trying the same thing over and over and expecting different results."*

Difficulties in our life are often tests. Our circumstances are like equations with a missing component and we have to figure out the problem in order to pass the test. Try different approaches to areas where you are stuck. Ask questions of people who have conquered the challenge you struggle with. Victory is often just one step away, yet figuring out that one step—and taking it—is the essence of what it means to win in life and in your career.

I am told if you put a frog in a pot and put a lid on it, the frog will try to jump out and hit the lid many times; yet finally, the frog will stop. Then if you take the lid off, the frog still will not jump out, because he has been trained he cannot. It is similar to cows and an electric fence; once they have been shocked a few times, they will not touch the fence even when it is turned off. They have been conditioned to accept this limitation. What training holds you back from achieving greater things? Have you hit your head so many times that you are afraid to jump? What limitation have you accepted that you could really get beyond? Have you allowed life's shocks to stop you from trying?

I do not advocate being foolish. Only you can determine areas where you might be holding yourself back, instead of observing a legitimate obstacle. But keep looking for solutions. Dare yourself to keep trying. Your limitations may be self-imposed and you may be able to grow far beyond what you currently believe is possible. Do not "sell yourself short."

I remember at ten years old, entering the citywide *Punt, Pass, and Kick* football competition. I practiced relentlessly. Yet the day of the event, they were not going to let me compete because I had jumped and landed on a barbed wire fence and developed a nasty puncture wound on my leg. But I refused to accept their limitation and sold the officials on why I was okay to compete. When I returned from having my leg sewn up, I learned I was the champion for my age division. I am glad I sold myself and those contest officials on my ability to compete. Instead of accepting their limitations, I pressed on and accomplished something great. You, too, can sell your way past many of your limitations—if you will truly try. *"If at first you don't succeed; try, try again"* (Thomas H. Palmer, Teacher's Manual of 1840).

❧❀❧

Action Required

1. Be sharp. Have a good attitude. Listen. Learn. Be a problem solver.

2. Identify one area in which you have limited yourself. Try these techniques to overcome that difficulty. Write down your results for at least one week to make sure you are trying.

Phrase to Memorize

"I will not sell myself short."

MAKE TODAY GREAT

EXPONENTIAL IDEA 10

Hearing the Music

Key Idea

Even if Life has Many Days, it is too Short to Live Without Happiness

Our life should be a song that finds the harmonies in life.

Nothing motivates people more than the power of music. Rock songs stir people into a frenzy. Romantic melodies move hearts towards love. Bands electrify crowds to cheer for their team. Fight songs move the "Rockys" of the world to prevail in difficult contests. Songs like "Chariots of Fire" inspire athletes to run farther and faster than ever before. Songs like "America the Beautiful" can turn people's thoughts toward patriotism. In short, music is a powerful motivational tool!

If we are in tune in our faith, work, play, and outlook, then our life will produce a harmonic tone. Lives that are out of synch and full of mayhem, produce notes of discord. While vital, clean, and productive lives generate a harmonious, appealing sound.

What kind of sounds are you producing in the flow of your own life? Sometimes we forget to play the music. You cannot experience the transforming power of a song without singing the notes. To maximize your life you must capture and celebrate the beautiful notes of your journey. Is your switch turned off or are you turned on and tuned in?

Maybe the music in your world sounds sour and out of tune right now. That's okay. We all need "tune-ups." You may need to look for the sounds of good in your life to find them. If you concentrate on the negative, you will never find the joyful notes of hope and goodness around you. To "tune-up," you must find and sing the high quality, good notes of your life. Brightness and harmony are not found by cursing the darkness but by turning on the light. You may have to turn the channel to find your right song.

Just like it is possible to miss a turn on a road trip, it is possible to miss the music in living. In a real sense, finding the missing music in your life is like finding your way after a wrong turn. Sometimes it even requires a change of course to find your way. Rediscover the song in your life and see if you do not sense you are pointed in a better direction.

Sometimes people are way too figurative and do not take good advice literally enough to experience its truth. Music is that way. Talking about it will not produce its good. Start singing. It is more than a metaphor. Hum. Whistle. Play an instrument. Be upbeat. Look to make your life a melody. Find ways to make your life, career, and play be full of glorious notes. Sing your song in life.

Florence Littauer said, *"Don't die with the music still in you"* (influenced from a quote of Oliver Wendell Holmes in *The Voiceless*, 1858). What powerful advice! Inside each one of us is a harmony, a tune, a message—something only we can share. We each have our own uniqueness that needs to be expressed. Nothing will completely satisfy you, until you share this tune of your life. Live up to your highest potential. With God's help, sing your highest notes of achievement in the way you live your life.

Sadly, it is possible to go through life and never discover the music that resonates with your soul. You can exist without ever strumming a chord. You must choose to see your life as a song. It is not a requirement. You must choose to paint the artistry of your life to find it. Let this be the moment you wake up to discover the joyous sounds playing within you.

It is up to you. No one will make your music for you. Choose to sing, instead of crying. Find the worth. Find the beauty. Look for the good. Let your whole life be imbued with meaning. Instead of focusing on the bad, listen deeply for the melodious sounds reverberating in your soul. Let your life's song be so clear, everyone can hear the music within you.

❧❦

Action Required

Music is a powerful motivator. Write down at least one way you can use music as a tool to help you achieve more. (Examples: exercise, relationships, work career, rest, etc.)

Phrase to Memorize

"The way I live; this is my song."

MAKE TODAY GREAT

EXPONENTIAL IDEA 11

Work and Hunting

Key Idea

We Only Find Life's Treasures When We Seek Them with Purpose and Deliberate Intent

❧❧

All people have differing interests and this is good. I know many of you have zero interest in hunting. Still, I refer to hunting as a pursuit that has taught me great lessons: lessons that are valuable in every area of life, whether you like hunting or not. So let's consider twelve lessons I have learned from the hunt.

47

Lesson #1: In Good Seasons and in Bad, Keep Hunting

You will never learn the art sitting on the porch. You must be in the woods. Likewise, in work and life, you cannot prevail without consistent effort. If you do not try, you cannot win. If it is a task worth doing then it is worth pursuing diligently. To master any task, you must stay in the hunt.

Lesson #2: Always Maintain a Sharp Eye

It is amazing how much we fail to see. Many matters that critically influence our life and career slip right by us. Learn to be a better student of the game. Reducing the missed clues and signals will help us make fewer mistakes and win more often.

Lesson #3: You Don't Even Know the Ones that "Get Away"

This may seem to be a restatement of Lesson #2, but the point is so important, it deserves expansion. The scariest prospect of missed opportunities is that they do not announce themselves. If we are not paying attention in "alert mode," many of the possibilities in life walk right by, without our discovery.

Lesson #4: Sleeping in the Stand can Cost You Big Bucks

Inattentiveness rarely produces the best results. A little luck never hurts, but our chances always improve if we stay wide awake and pay attention to our surroundings.

Lesson #5: Aim for the Heart

You will never hit the bull's-eye aiming for the edge of the target. Define what it is you are after and aim for it with all of your might. Focus on the very essence of what you want to achieve. Take steady aim at the heart of what you want. Direct all of your energy towards achieving the exact center of what you are after. Clarify your target and shoot for the bull's-eye.

Lesson #6: Take Care of Your Weapon

What a disappointing day it is to watch the "one" you have been hunting for scamper through the woods . . . getting away only because the weapon's scope was not zeroed in on the target, or the weapon misfires because it was not properly maintained. Whatever your tools in your work or trade, they require maintenance. If you don't take care of your skills and the tools of your trade, they cannot take care of you. Don't get so busy looking for the target that you forget to maintain the tools that will help you obtain it. An ounce of prevention is worth a pound of cure. Take care of the things that you count on to take care of you.

Lesson #7: Use Good Ammunition

I cannot count the number of times cutting corners has cost me the thing I was hunting. It is better to invest in good ammunition in the first place. Excellent goods and services are not properly marketed with cheap or inferior materials. Good customers are not obtained or cared for with haphazard components or service. The quality of the catch is often determined by the strength of the means we use to obtain it. How many a fisherman has lamented that the big one got away, knowing well that he only has himself to blame, since the prize fish escaped only because low test or frayed line broke during the fight to land the catch? To ensure you maximize your possibilities of winning the hunt (whether the quarry is wildlife or a business prospect), use good ammunition. In the professional realm, your ammunition is your equipment and supplies. Your quality will improve if your materials do.

Lesson #8: Study Your Prey

I am an avid deer hunter, but I was not raised to be one. I had to learn the art. I spent a whole season running a wildlife check-in station at Ocala National Forest in Florida. I did this just to learn more about the woods, animals, and one animal in particular—deer. They are amazing animals with an acute sense of smell, unique visual senses, great hearing abilities, and amazing talents of physical speed and coordination.

You might get lucky once or twice, but you will not successfully hunt this incredible animal without knowing a lot about them. The same is true in our careers and life pursuits. We are unlikely to capture our desired goal unless we know a lot about the subject. Study your marketplace. Study your customers. Study your skill set. Study the very thing you are after. You will greatly increase your chances of success if you become a student of the game you want to win.

Lesson #9: Take Your Best Shot Every Time

Haphazard shots only waste ammunition, wound prey, and frustrate feelings. If you want to perform, a weak audition will lose you the stage. If you want to sing, a poor song will lose you the audience. If you want to land the right job, a lackluster interview will lose you the opportunity. You have to put the cross hairs on what you want, and steady your shot, if you want to win at what you do. Learn to give perfect performances. As the clarified saying goes, *"Perfect practice makes perfect."*

I have taught karate for many years, and I teach my students it is not rote memory, but exact execution that increases skill. Often, I won't teach the next technique until the first one is mastered. Excellence is not built on sloppy performance. Always deliver the product you yourself would like to receive and you will find yourself advancing in what you do and how you do it. Do not waste time or energy on untrained effort. Practice doing what you do with great delivery. Take your best shot.

Lesson #10: Let the Little Ones Walk

Greed is an undesirable quality. It is alright to let the little ones get away. In fact, it is better. Have you ever seen someone trying to eat little bitty, bony fish? Unless you are starving to death, it is best to throw them back. There isn't much meat— only a whole lot of bones and waste.

You can't be ready for the "big one" if you spend all of your time and energy on "little ones." It's a good thing to let some get away. It will train your senses to pay attention to what you are shooting at and to focus your energies on the ones you really want to catch. The best hunters and fishermen let some get away on purpose, but rarely miss when the right one comes along. Learn to be selective.

Lesson #11: Enjoy the Hunt, Even When You Don't Bring Home a Catch

Some of my most enjoyable hunts have been when I didn't shoot a thing. Getting so still, I evoke the curiosity of a squirrel to come right up to me, to see what kind of thing I am; and I see myriads of animals, birds, bugs, and things I would never see if I wasn't there hunting, no matter the score. Learn to enjoy your surroundings. Appreciate the things around you. Become alive to your environment. Enjoy the hunt, even when you don't shoot. Enjoy the fishing trip, even when they aren't biting. Enjoy your job, even when you have "off" days. Learning to appreciate the whole of your life will make you really enjoy it when you score big.

Lesson #12: Be Thankful for Your Catch

If you snag a client but they don't feel appreciated, see how many of their friends and neighbors they tell. It is easy to rush by a winning moment without really feeling gratitude. This is called "missing the moment." When you win, give thanks for your abilities. Give thanks for your job or opportunity. Give thanks for your customer. Jesus healed ten on a certain occasion and only one returned to give thanks. Be the one. Be sure to recognize, appreciate, and acknowledge the goodness that comes your way. You will find all your hunts may then become more rewarding.

❧❧

Action Required

Be an intentional hunter. Name three specific things you want to learn to do better—in your career or personal life. How will you become a better student of the game and develop these goals? Write them down and review your list once a week for the next year. Put them in your electronic calendar or written organizer as a reminder.

Phrases to Memorize

1. Aim for the heart. Aim for the bull's-eye.

2. Sleeping in the stand could cost you "big bucks."

MAKE TODAY GREAT

EXPONENTIAL IDEA 12

Be a Doer

Key Idea

Perhaps No Lesson About Improving Our Life has More Profound Professional and Practical Applications than Learning to "Be a Doer"

❧❧

Recently, my wife went through the annual task of preparing a huge Thanksgiving meal for our family and friends. The experience of the festive gathering and the time of sharing food and fellowship was certainly a blessing worth her hard work and sacrifice. This year was particularly special, because it was the first time our ten-month old grandson, Jaxson, could join us. He certainly brought mirth and joy to an already special occasion.

After everyone had left and the merriment had ended, the daunting task of cleaning up still remained. Even though my sweet wife was exhausted from staying up the night before in order to do the cooking and make the decorative preparations, she was still going to finish cleaning up before heading to bed. Seeing her exhaustion, I told her to go to bed. I volunteered to put up the celebration food remnants for her.

When I surveyed the living room and kitchen, it was evident that much more would need to be done than simply putting up the food. I knew my sweetheart would have to spend her entire day after Thanksgiving cleaning, so I considered doing the monumental task for her. However, the prospect seemed overwhelming and I didn't even know where to begin. Therefore, I decided to start with one task at a time and see how much I could accomplish. The completion of each task was noticeable and gratifying, so I just kept doing one more task at a time, and realized the job was more manageable than I had initially thought. Yet, I only discovered this as I began to work on it.

The next morning when my wife awoke, she had the pleasure of looking at a sparkling living room and kitchen. Instead of spending her day cleaning up holiday hoopla, she was able to do other things. The point is, had I not decided to *do* something about it, my wife would have not been able to enjoy her day off.

Doing something about conditions that need change in our lives is as crucial to success and happiness, as fuel is to combustion. We can see areas that deserve our efforts, but like the leftover Thanksgiving feast, these can seem overwhelming. Often, only engaging in the task of addressing these issues will reveal the steps to overcoming them.

Simply *saying* we want to change is no more effective than telling our car to start without inserting and turning the key!

My wife and I have three teenagers living in our home. If you don't know what "lip service" means, just ask teens to do work around the house. You will get lots of *"OKs," "Yes Ma'ams,"* and *"Yes Sirs,"* and subsequently, a whole bunch of finding out the requested job was never done. Saying we will do something is only step one. The old saying accurately declares: *"Talk is cheap."*

The most important component of turning ideals into reality is well-aimed action. Old farmers will tell you, *"You can't turn any field over in your mind."* The only way to reap a harvest is to actually till the soil, plant the seeds, and actively pull the weeds and tend the plants.

You must develop a "habit of doing." This requires you to follow up your talk with actions. The action habit requires practice. You must do something about the things with which you are concerned. If you become more active in addressing challenges, you might surprise yourself. One healthy effort leads to another. You can build a chain reaction of positive, reinforcing behaviors. The more you *do* about a problem, the more you discover additional efforts you can *do* and you develop the belief that you can overcome.

For years, I have used a "To-Do" list. These lists are great as long as they lead to action. If lists just get longer and longer and very little gets crossed off, then they are not effective. For the last couple of years, I have used "Done" lists to monitor and work on my professional and personal performance. They focus on what I am actually getting done vs. what I am *saying* I need to do. What have you "Done" recently to improve your life and career? Yes, identify what you need to do but make it a point to turn those things into completed tasks.

As a matter of fact, a "To Do" list can be limiting. If you are not also focusing on the issues at hand, you will miss out on opportunities to be more productive. Dare to look in the mirror. Give yourself a lecture if it is needed. I often do. Whatever it takes; make sure you are actively working on areas of your life you need to enhance.

Becoming a doer involves a solid approach to life's circumstances. Here's a good illustration. As a teacher of Shotokan karate for many years, I have my students focus on crucial fundamentals—like Vince Lombardi's "This is a Football" talk. (If you have not heard of this talk, it is very important. Google it.) In teaching karate, I teach that one of the most important foundation points of good Shotokan is a solid stance. Thus, I rigorously train my students to have a good base. I also instruct them to be able to move their base forward, backwards, or to either side—with ease and reflex. They must have a "ready" stance to be able to execute techniques in conflict.

Similarly, we must have a good foundation to win. Life requires us to have a "ready" stance to meet our obstacles. We need to have a prepared state of mind that is "ready" for action.

We must be "ready" "to do" what is needed to survive and thrive in our personal and work dimensions. Just talking about it is not enough. We must act as needed to achieve results. We must have a foundation of "being a doer."

❧❧

Action Required

Identify a situation in your life that needs some correction. Even if you do not know all the steps, start moving forward. You will never succeed if you don't start.

Phrase to Memorize

"I can build a chain of positive, reinforcing behavior that will help me overcome adversity."

MAKE TODAY GREAT

EXPONENTIAL IDEA 13

Daily Commitment

Key Idea

Life is a Daily Task . . . You Cannot Live on Yesterday's Laurels or Tomorrows Dreams

What you do today is important, every day! You cannot ignore the opportunities of the present and live your best life. Life is right now. Life is today!

❧❧

Life is moments, brief moments . . .
Be they lost or be they gain.
One thing for sure, we shall not pass this way again.
Moments, yes that's all you have—
Brief moments so fleeting.
Do not rush by them on your way to a meeting!

How do we get the most out of today? At work and at home, how do we get the best from our lives? The suggestions here will help you get the most out of your life. Some of them overlap, as truth's often do. You will have to do the work to apply these powerful concepts to your own life.

1. *Be Results Driven*

It is easy to be overwhelmed by influences, and miss outcomes. It is possible to worry so much about what people think, that you miss the results you are aiming for. Be passionate about achieving your own priorities.

One of the chief culprits of achieving results is the presence of worry. We cannot achieve maximum results if we are burdened down by worry.

"Don't Worry, Be Happy," the song childishly goes (song authored by Bobby McFerrin and sung by Bob Marley), or is it childish?

Worry really is a performance zapper! You cannot achieve your best today if you are controlled by worry. Therefore let it go so you can do your best.

The illustration on the following page will help you to see why worrying is completely pointless.

Slam's "Don't Worry" Model

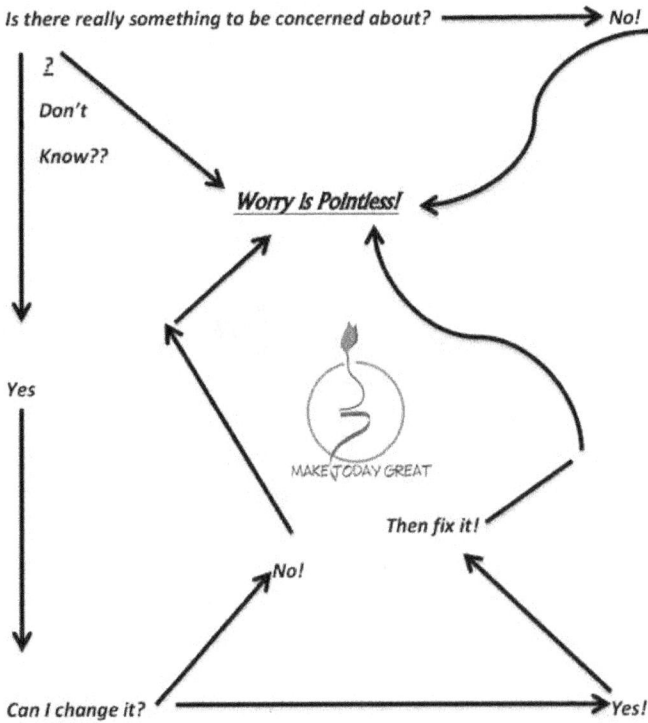

Is there really something to be concerned about? ⟶ **No!**

?

Don't

Know??

Worry Is Pointless!

Yes

MAKE TODAY GREAT

Then fix it!

No!

Can I change it? ⟶ Yes!

As I mentioned earlier, I teach Shotokan karate. This is a very results-driven pursuit. In teaching my students, I regularly remind them that their greatest contest is with themselves. That is why it is important for them to be aware of the real facts about their technique level, and the degree of improvements needed to advance.

The best professionals are able to take this martial arts perspective into their workplace. They remind themselves that they are always in a contest with themselves to improve, and in so doing, they stay in touch daily with the real facts about their performance.

Be in touch with your performance. Be *results driven*!

2. *Face Your Difficulties with Courage*

It is amazing how failing to face an area of challenge can inflate it in your mind. Avoidance tactics actually make the problem harder to deal with. Facing things squarely tends to make them look smaller, while failing to face them makes them look bigger. Daily commitment starts by facing facts now!

It takes courage to face difficulties because the truth is that we all make mistakes. Facing our difficulties demands that we own up to these defects. That is where excellence begins. The threshold of honesty with ourselves in our professional and personal assessments is the critical foundation of a solid life and career. Honest business is good business. Therefore, you must face your difficulties with courage.

3. *Take Direct, Clear Action*

Another power principle of Shotokan is a linear strategy. The old axiom is that the shortest distance between two points is a straight line. Shotokan drives this into students with every technique. I mention this because this concept is also true in business and life. A straight linear strategy is very effective.

I used to have a problem of overcomplicating situations. Analysis can be an excuse for paralysis. Planning is important, but it is also important not to let your thinking be an excuse for inaction. Meet your problems head on!

4. *Smile and Wait*

Think first rather than pushing ahead and regretting your decision. This is not double talk but balance. I am an advocate for action, except when it is highly questionable what the next right action should be. In this case, do not compound your lack of information by piling a mistake on top of it.

The day is always better when you move toward strength and purpose. That is why I have learned to write difficult notes to people and then save them as a draft. Sometimes, I send them the next day, just like I initially wrote them. Sometimes, I send them in a few days, after changing them. And sometimes, after further review, I become very glad I never sent them at all. When you feel uneasy about something today, it may be that your second thought will be your best thought. Not everything has to be dealt with today! Deal with those things that you know you should. Come back to those things about which you need clarity.

Today: think first, before you hit send!

5. *There is a Time to Quit Thinking About it and Move On!*

Reason can be the process of being solid and sound-minded. It can also be the process of being wimpy, excuse-driven, and un-motivated. When you have done your homework, thought about it, and prayed about it, then quit thinking about it and do it! Think first but don't think too much! Do not get stuck in lethargy. Know when to let go and move on!

In conclusion, life is a daily deal. You must shower, dress, eat, exercise, work, play, and rest some every day. There are many daily tasks. Take none for granted. Be performance-oriented. You cannot skip a day and you cannot bring a single day back. Make a commitment. Give your best to each day!

❧❧

Action Required

How can you be more results driven, face your difficulties with courage, take clear action, and move on in your life? Identify three conditions that need improvement in your daily life. Write down ideas on how to improve them. Even if you do not know the whole solution, begin to take definite steps to work on them. You will never succeed if you don't start. Start today.

Phrase to Memorize

"I can make a daily commitment to improve. Each day, I can build a link in a chain of positive, reinforcing behavior that will help me overcome adversity and have a better life."

MAKE TODAY GREAT

EXPONENTIAL IDEA 14

Course Correction

Key Idea

If We Always Made the Right Decisions in the First Place and Did the Right Things from the Beginning, there Would be Zero Self-Improvement

But . . . that's not the way personal experience or professional careers go, in real life. Where we are, is seldom the ideal of where we want to be. Because of this, one of the biggest needs for growth in our life is to be able to adjust our course, to achieve more and be more.

❧❧

My friend Steve Gutzler first called me "Slam" thirty-five years ago and I have lived up to my name during the course of my life.

69

I used to be like one of those bulls you hear about in a china shop. This sounds funny but in many ways it is true. I was always moving and going hard: salesman extraordinaire, outdoorsman, karate fighter, preacher, and hot pepper connoisseur—I have lived anything but a boring life.

Yet, even with me, there have been periods of time that I have let complacency set in. That in fact, is one of the major things that cause us to need course corrections in our lives. If we are not careful, the stresses of life can cause the strongest of us to let apathy creep in the door. And this is a condition deadly to growth. Lethargy in life is like mold on bread; it makes it unfit for use and benefit.

The bone-shattering truth is that change must be in the cards for us. If we are to remain relevant and effective in our professional and personal performance, we must grow. We must change. When and how to change—that is the million dollar question. Here are some acid tests, to help us see if the changes in our lives are the kind of changes we need.

Acid Test Number 1

What is our motive? Are we changing for good? We don't need change for the sake of change. We need change for the attainment of better lives and careers. What is your motive? Do you need to change for good? Do not let vanity or poorly aimed pursuits rob you of your potential effectiveness. Make sure your changes are good changes.

Acid Test Number 2

Upon what is your plan of change being built? Are there experiences, guidance, resources, and personal strength in your background—strengths that make the changes you plan feasible, possible, and rewarding? Good change must be built on something. There must be a foundation. Roots must run deep if the tree is to grow tall! Good change must be built on something.

Acid Test Number 3

Does the change make sense with your current life? Many times, people attempt drastic change without a healthy vision, and that is not realistic. Most times, when we service our car, we change the oil, not the motor. Good changes are balanced and focused. They do not wreck our lives to execute them. They add to our lives, when carried out effectively.

So, we know we need to change to avoid apathy and lethargy. Yet to change wisely, we know we need a good motive. We know we need to build on our foundation. And we know that our proposed change needs to make sense, in our overall life. It is plainly clear that trying the same thing over and over and expecting different results is insanity. Thus, change we must. I charge you emphatically, to be willing to make a positive difference in your life. Make the change in your life that needs to be done!

If you have applied the acid test in the first part of this writing, I assume that you know what to do. I assume that motivation is not your problem, and that you are willing to make the changes you need to make. These things being true . . . then comes the thousand-pound gorilla question; how do we change? How do we improve our performance, to address the need we recognize?

Good question, and here are answers. Here are seven steps to help you make the changes you believe you should make. Seven basic ideas that will help you improve your performance when you recognize need.

Step #1: Realize the Area of Deficiency

Write it down. I remember one of the hardest deficiencies to correct in my selling performance was a tendency not to listen deeply enough. Through work and time, I replaced this tendency with a habit of active listening. But first I had to realize what I needed to change. I had to honestly admit it and be clear about what I wanted to fix, with a course correction. So in the same light, be honest with yourself. What is it you need to change?

Step #2: Identify the Corrective Behavior or Action

Write it down. Replace your negative with a positive. If you have a trait you do not like, then what is the trait you want to replace it with? It is very important that you do not generalize this. You must see specifically and know clearly the solution you need to build into your life. Change made without clearly identifying the replacement ideal will be short-lived and will not last. What is the outcome you seek?

Step #3: Recognize the Moments When You Need to Change

Arresting a problem area of your life is like going after a rabbit. First you have to catch it, and it will not stay still. How do you catch the rabbit of your problem? Do you realize *when* you do the thing, you need to change? (Are you self-aware enough to recognize the things that need changing?)

Learning to sense the moment when change is needed is half the battle. When your attention is sought in a department store, often they will flash the lights. That grabs our attention. When attention is needed in school, they will ring a bell. That grabs our attention. Sometimes, to make sure we get it, an announcement is made on the intercom. That really drives the point home.

This is what we need to do at the moment when change is needed. We need to let the lights flash. We need to let the bells ring. We need to make an announcement to ourselves. This is it! This is the pregnant moment when we are looking at what we need to do differently. Recognize the moment, when change is needed.

Step #4: Have a Moment of Heightened Consciousness

When we realize the moment when change is needed, remember, you have won half the battle. Seize the moment. Carpe Diem. Consciously think the replacement ideal. Be crystal clear that now is your moment of opportunity. See it for what it is. It is no longer a moment of inadequacy but a new moment of growth. Turn the channel in your mind on the old thought or practice and replace it with the new thought or action.

Step #5: Act Upon the Realization

Consciously practice the desired trait, performance, or behavior. Do the desired change. Fill the void of the old pursuit with your intended new course of action. Practice the new, meaningful directed action, at the very moment where you were tempted to do the old thing.

Work on the new behavior or purpose, with each moment of realization.

Step #6: Repeat the Cycle Until Your Course is Corrected

Les Brown said it best; *"It's not over till I win."* And it's not. You are not after a one-time change but a renewed mind and performance. Practice and keep practicing the change you seek, until it becomes a habit. Repeat the positive cycle.

Be patient with yourself. Just like the old ideology or problem did not happen overnight, effecting real, lasting change will not happen suddenly. Keep on keeping on—practicing this process—until the change you seek has become ingrained as a way of life!

Step #7: Note Your Success!

Reward yourself. More specifically, reinforce the change you have affected in your life with positive gratification. Go do something special! Have a private victory dance! Mark the moment! Celebrate the victory of your course correction with an internal *"Atta-Boy"* or *"Atta-Girl"* and an external observance to mark the moment.

A good example of this is found in the Old Testament. Here, patriarchs and leaders of the people marked special events in their lives with an altar. They made a place of remembrance that caused themselves and others to see the good thing that happened there. Even so, build altars of gratitude when you effect positive changes in your life with the help of your Higher Power. If you do, the changes will likely mean more and last longer.

❧❧

Action Required

Believe you can change with good motives, foundation, and realism. Realize, identify, and recognize changes you need to make. Seize your moment of opportunity; act at the moment needed. Repeat the cycle as long as it takes, and celebrate your victory.

Phrase to Memorize

"I commit to improve this day. Today, I will build a link in a chain of positive, reinforcing behavior. I will grow and change to have a better life."

MAKE TODAY GREAT

EXPONENTIAL IDEA 15

The Second Mile

Key Idea

The Power to Prevail and Win is Often Generated by a Strong Finish

A great deal is said about the importance of strong starts. This is one of the most popular ideas among positive thinkers. Just as important but not as popular is the notion of a strong finish. Many a great start from the tee in the game of golf, is made sour by poor performance on the green. The finish is as critical as the start. In fact, the best starts start with a great finish in mind.

❧❧

The greatest ideas are most often proposed by the greatest leaders. That is why I pay most careful attention to the Master

77

Teacher, Jesus. One of the wise teachings of Christ is His command, *"If your neighbor asks you to go with him a mile, go with him two"* (Matthew 5:41). This thinking seems reverse of the way most people approach life. Give the least you can in a situation and get the most out of it seems to be the popular approach. Jesus points out a higher wisdom. Give the most you can in a situation and you will naturally get the best out of it. Call it karma. Call it the law of the harvest. Call it whatever. But a mindset to give more than what is required will bring more bountiful results. That is the lesson here.

We like to do something and be done with it. Yet, the most important matters in life nearly always require second effort. Dr. Denis Waitley, in teaching this concept, asks a whole room of people to raise their hand as high as they can. Then when they do, he immediately follows with the command, *"Now raise your hand higher."* Without exception, everyone in the room raises their hand even higher than they did the first time. Why? It is because we seldom give our best to first efforts. We can nearly always raise the bar a little higher and try a little harder.

Remember Rocky? I like to call his winning power "The Rocky Syndrome." What do I mean by this? I mean a guy who refuses to go down is really hard to beat. As a karate teacher, I know this to be true. Giving that added oomph, the extra effort at the finish line that the opponent does not expect, sets you apart from the competition.

When I was a young boy, a gang of boys came after me on bicycles and knocked me off my bike. I was on my way home after Little League football practice. They hit me, spit on me, ridiculed me, and humiliated me. Most were older boys and I didn't stand a chance against all twenty or more of them.

After I was thoroughly distraught and crying, they seemed to have had enough fun and let me go. But as I rode off, they changed their minds. In an old gravel parking lot, they knocked me down again and continued to terrify and torment me.

My world seemed to end. I was horror stricken to be so despicably used by a gang of boys I would still have to face every day at school. I'd be branded a coward. Then a wonderful thing happened. I saw from the ground my father's old station-wagon drive around the corner at the Old Amazon Cotton Mill. My dad wondered where I was and came to check on me.

My heart skipped with joy as I said to myself, *"Here comes the rescue squad! Here comes the rescue squad!"*As my father pulled his vehicle over beside the curb, you never saw a bunch of boys scatter as fast as those boys did from the tight knit circle around me. My dad looked like a mountain coming out of the vehicle, and he was obviously in no mood to play.

He dared the boys to move and slowly took off his belt. Then he asked me which boy had beaten me up! It had been several, but I picked the biggest, oldest, meanest boy who had been the cruelest to me. Elated to point him out, I said, "*It was him dad*!" Then unexpectedly, my father turned his steel-blue eyes to mine and said, *"Son, do you want to fight him or me?"* My delight turned fast—to resolve, because I knew my dad wasn't kidding, and if I had to pick between that grade school ruffian and my father, my choice was clear. Let me at him! At least now it would be one on one.

I jumped on the bigger, older boy. Everybody claimed he won the fight, because of my bloody nose. I just know my father finally stopped the fight when I had the better hand of the boy and my dad felt it necessary to pull me off the top of him. So, on a day when my little world would have been shattered, my dignity was restored. By teaching me to fight for myself and making me face my own challenges, my father did far more for me than he could have by coming to my aid and rescuing me.

Instead of looking at my shoes in shame the next day at school, I held my head high. My father had helped me earn self-respect and the respect of the other boys. I never forgot that lesson. It serves me well, even today. Lessons like this teach us courage and responsibility, and while difficult at the time, they are the stuff of breakthroughs and overcoming lives.

Sometimes, it's just a bit extra that causes the scale to tip up, not down. I ran for many years, and learned that when it gets difficult, you can almost always get a second wind. It seems the power to finish resides within us. But the power to finish does not run to the finish line . . . it runs *past* the finish line.

Babe Ruth struck out a lot. Still, he is not remembered as the strike out king but the home run king. People will forgive and forget your limitations if you rise above them, to win. Keep swinging. Make it a habit to finish strong. Always do a little more than expected. Let your personal trademark be that you exceed requirements. Give more than you have to. You will find that finishing strong will increase your ability to win, personally and professionally.

❧❧

Action Required

Shortcuts can shortchange your life. Look for ways to go the second mile. Look for ways to stretch your performance beyond your current thresholds. What are some ways you will now try renewed second efforts, and to finish stronger?

Phrase to Memorize

The finish is as critical as the start. In fact, the best starts, start with a great finish in mind.

MAKE TODAY GREAT

EXPONENTIAL IDEA 16

Sew Good Stitches—Personal Values

Key Idea

We Must Know the Value of Our Work for it to be Fulfilling

We must believe that our work is good and that what we stand for is being expressed through what we do. Having defining values that matter and letting them guide our steps can turn life from frustrating, to joyous and happy.

❧❧

Whenever I wanted a hero, I never had to look any further than home; my father always was one. *John W. Carter Sr.* and *value* were congruent terms.

We kept a sports chest in my home. Balls and gear were handed down from my brother to me. Then they were repaired by a father, who made everything last as long as it could.

For instance, we had a family Spaulding football. Today, it is approximately fifty years old and in good repair. But it was not always this way. My brother and I literally wore it out. So much so, that the stitches went away.

I will never forget my father taking that football into his shop and painstakingly making new laces from shoe strings that he dipped in some type of special coating. These laces were so artfully installed that the ball was made literally better than new, especially after my father treated the leather. His work was so extraordinary that even after years of me playing with it, it is still in great shape today.

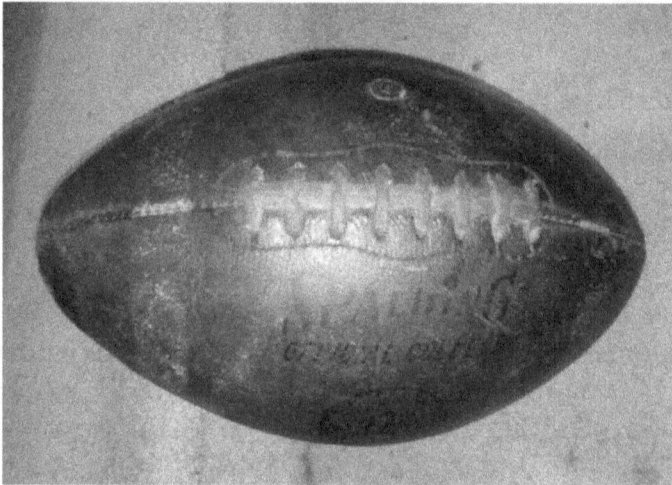

John W. Carter Sr. knew the meaning of work and value. He knew his stitches would be good and that they would last. I try to remember his example in my job performance, even now, sixteen years after his passing. Am I doing good work? Is it work of value? Am I sewing stitches that will last?

We sew good stitches by living according to our values. I have spent quite some time defining my values. Some of them are:

1. Being faithful to and sharing Christ's love

2. Being true to my wife

3. Being faithful to my friends

4. Helping people recover from substance abuse

5. Standing up for the weak and the underdog

6. Being a sought-after speaker on inspirational and sales topics

7. Pursuing and winning at a professional game-plan to increase my income

8. Patriotic duty to the constitutionally governed United States of America

9. Pursuing Quaker values

10. Gardening, carpentry, and outdoor work

11. Nature, hunting, and fishing

12. Continuing to write and create

13. Teaching Shotokan karate

14. Staying involved to inspire young people

15. Having fun and enjoying life

These things are important to me. If I follow them rigorously in my life's game-plan, I will be successful. I will sew good stitches, like my father. What are your values? You must know them to know how to sew your own good stitches.

Last year a friend and I, Gio Gaudelli, had a conversation about a man who inspires us both. Our chat started when Gio quoted Will Rogers saying: *"The worst thing that happens to you may be the best thing for you if you don't let it get the best of you."*

Will Rogers was one of the greatest figures in American communications history. As Gio said: *"He is on my WOW list!"* Sadly, though he was perhaps the greatest spokesman for the country, almost no one today has heard of him. Still, his sense of humor and his great sense of perspective were unparalleled. He had a powerful sense of great, personal value.

> *"He was like Lincoln or Twain, only better. (They did meet people they didn't like, and they couldn't throw a lasso.) He took care not to offend or challenge core beliefs and he allowed his listeners to continue to think that common sense and two-syllable words could get to the heart of any problem"* (pg. xiii of Introduction: Will Rogers Biography, by Ben Yagoda).

Will Rogers was an Indian, cowboy, and vaudeville star, and in an amazing way captured the soul of America enough to be its worldwide spokesperson. He had a great sense of perspective and value.

He took the variety of experiences that comprised his background and communicated them in the healthiest view possible. If we can follow his example and take the myriad of influences around us and see them the rightly, we can optimize our personal vision and fulfillment.

The greatest gift we have is our own experience. Using these experiences to come to the right outlook and view of things makes our lives healthy, well, and productive. Our experiences can give us a great sense of value! They give us the correct perspective about what has happened in our lives.

How do we get such a perspective of value? How do we change from status quo to energized soul? How do we assess our lives differently and improve the way we look at things and thereby perform?

The good news is that you probably already know the answer to this, on some level. God does not play hide-and-seek regarding the major purposes of life. And He does not make the prospect of finding our own healthy outlook an impossible guessing game.

To find our own healthy value, we do have to learn. We do have to seek. But we do not have to worry. We will find our "right" way, if we open the channels and honestly search. If we are faithful to do this, we will find our answers. More than that, our answers will find us!

Surely, you have values, the values that can lead you to a better life. What are they? Only you can answer that question for yourself . . . and answer it you must, so you can advance towards greater fulfillment and performance.

As I stated earlier, I worked for one of the best friends I have had in this life, Wolfgang Hafele. He is deceased now. But the lessons he taught me live on. I will never forget Wolfgang saying "*I know that I don't know.*"

Wolfgang's ability to look at a situation as if it was brand new, transformed the way I look at value. As I shared back in *Exponential Idea 4*, Wofgang looked past how something had been done before, and saw things from a totally fresh, almost child-like perspective. Solving each problem in business was obviously an adventure that he enjoyed.

I miss Wolfgang, and yet I still benefit from this lesson he taught me. He had a great sense of perspective and value. His powerful problem-solving trait must be the beginning of growth. We cannot even begin, until we have an open mind and heart. We must adopt an optimistic openness that believes there can be *even higher value* than the best way it has been done before.

Because of this powerful outlook, Wolfgang solved many "impossible" situations. We can do the same if we do not get so entrenched in our positions that we cannot learn. To improve our perspective, we must start with a fresh approach each day.

Clear your mind and heart, and open yourself to new vistas of learning, outlook, and attitude. Start with the internal value that you believe you can make a difference, and follow through until you do.

❧❦

Action Required

As John W. Carter Sr., Will Rogers, and Wolfgang Hafele demonstrated, we can greatly enhance our lives by a great sense of value. And here is how we can do it:

* Start with a good, open-minded approach.
* Believe in improvement from the beginning.
* Know your own values and let them guide you.
* Sew good stitches.

Phrases to Memorize

1. We sew good stitches by living according to our values.

2. *"The worst thing that happens to you may be the best thing for you if you don't let it get the best of you."* -Will Rogers

EXPONENTIAL IDEA 17

Lessons of a Tire Gauge—
Improving Performance

Key Idea

Taking Ideas and Molding Them into Real Parts of Our Life and Performance is the Difference Between Being a Dreamer and an Achiever

To win in our lives and careers, we need specific ways to turn our good thoughts into actions and reality.

❧

I love simple things that work. As a Quaker, this is an indispensable part of me. "Slamism" is all about simple, power-packed strategies that make a difference in your life.

A simple mechanical thing that works is a tire gauge. Pop it on the tire and the gauge tells you how much pressure the tire needs. It's easy to use and effective to produce results. This is the kind of approach that we need to grow and develop in our lives. So, a tire gauge really has a lot to teach us about improvement.

Lesson #1

Before we even decide to measure the air in a tire, we must see that it is flat or at least needing inflation. This is the launching pad to personal change and development. Are we honest with ourselves? Can we admit areas that need change or improvement? This is crucial to lasting success in our lives and careers.

Lesson #2

One of the keys to using a tire gauge is actually having one when you need it. Knowing they exist doesn't help you much when you suspect you need air. Keeping one in the car or toolbox is the answer. Then it is there when you need it.

Personal improvement is like this also. We need assessment tools. For instance, New Year's Resolutions are an example of this, if they are regularly used with some consistency. Vision boards, work journals, data charts, quarterly reviews, and accountability partners are other examples of effective performance measurement tools we can use. The point is not to know what they are but to actually identify which ones work for you. Then employ them in your targeting, visioning, and purposing.

Lesson #3

Having the tool will do you no good if you don't know how to use it. You must know how to apply the assessment tool. This is necessary to turn theory into application: blue sky, into real life.

The best way to make sure you know how to use your measurement devices is to practice with them. Practice applying your assessment tools in your life and career. Test market them in your situation and see which one's work best for you.

Lesson #4

You must be able to accurately read the results. What is the tire gauge telling you? What are your assessment tools telling you? Don't get stuck in analysis paralysis, but it is absolutely necessary that you do your own regular personal and career inventories. You must have times and means where you read the results of your evaluation tools, to know how to grow.

Lesson #5

Look at the bigger picture. Get past the surface. Sometimes the tire does not just need air—it needs repair. It needs a patch. The only way you know this is if you let the information you have learned from the tire gauge cause correction.

Take a good look at what the underlying causes of the problem could be. Putting air in a leaky tire is not a good solution. Getting all pumped up about seeing your need is not good if you haven't taken a really good look at the best solution.

What is the underlying cause of your need to change? Detect the leaks (your non-effective habits) that lead to a loss of effectiveness.

Lesson #6

Know what you want the pressure to be. Often, even when people know the tire needs air, they do not fill it up to the correct pressure. This negatively affects the traction and the life of the tire.

Likewise, in our moves to improve our performance, if our desires to change are too nebulous or vague, we are not likely to achieve the results we hope for.

What is it that we hope for? What is the correct pressure? Have a clear idea of what you are after and you will have a much better chance of success. What you have measured will tell you where you are at. Knowing the desired result lets you know where you want to go. What is the difference between the two? If you know this, your chances of obtaining the desired result improve drastically.

Lesson #7

When the leaks are fixed, it is time to add the desired air pressure. This could be funding for a new business. This could be training for a new career move. This could be accountability through a partner for keeping on the course of action. It could be a lot of things. How will you add the pressure, i.e. force, to obtain your results? Tires don't fill themselves. Problems don't fix themselves. Don't think it to death. Get with it now that you know what to do. Add the right pressure to achieve your desired outcome.

Lesson #8

Test the results. Changes are seldom once-and-for-all. To make sure we really advance in our performance, the changes we make need ongoing checks and maintenance. Once you have solved this on the surface, what are the deeper levels to maintaining and maximizing this development?

You have to regularly check your tires—with a gauge. Decide before you begin the process that you will repeat it and look at your area of life-change again in the future.

Defining your method(s) of change should not only be a starting point but a measuring stick. When I was a little boy, my mother took a yardstick and made marks on the back of the closet door every so often to show me how I was growing. I loved this. You will feel better about your personal aiming if you measure up from time to time and see your progress and growth.

❧⸂❧

Action Required

Adopt simple ways to grow. Assess your situation, and apply tools to honestly measure it. Patch the problems. Add pressure to the solution. Test the results.

Phrases to Memorize

1. *"I will find and use simple, power packed strategies that make a difference in* my life."

2. We need specific ways we turn our good thoughts into actions and reality.

MAKE TODAY GREAT

EXPONENTIAL IDEA 18

Your Mountain is too Small

Key Idea

The Bigger the Problem, the Bigger the Solution Necessary to Overcome It

The bigger the task, the greater the advancement involved in going after it. Often people do not achieve, not because their talents are not good enough but because their targets are not high enough.

❧❧

In faith circles, when people are not shooting for goals worthy of their potential in life, I have heard the message, "*Your God is too small!*" I get the point, but there is a flip side to this truth. It is that their mountains are too small.

Who in their right mind would say, the problem behind a lack of victory is that the mountain of difficulty you face is not big enough? That crazy person would be me. I say that now and often, *"Your Mountain is too small!"*

Not long ago, my devoted friend of many years, Steve Gutzler, urged me to utilize "stretch" goals. To illustrate this, he shared with me about how he and one of his sons, believed God for really big answers to prayer, together. They did this as a father and son project, for forty days consecutively.

Steve went on to tell me that convincing answers were not immediately forthcoming from their efforts. In fact, things immediately seemed worse. Nevertheless, both of them remained faithful to believe for these "stretch" prayers to be answered. They kept their optimism, even though setbacks seemed more present than answers. Yet, after a little more than a year, amazing things began to happen and miraculous answers to their prayers were clearly provided. The mountain they faced seemed huge but they crossed it together, in faith and belief. Had they not tried, they would not have seen these marvelous developments.

Steve urged me to "stretch" myself to believe that God could accomplish bigger things than ever before in my life. So taking his words to heart, I began to "sleep on" these things. It is a very "Quaker" thing to "center" on what is really important. Therefore, when something really confronts and challenges me, I meditate on it. So I "chewed" on Steve's encouragement for me to do some "stretch" believing and praying.

After a time, a clear truth occurred to me. Sensing a higher calling has always "centered" and motivated me. When you believe there is something you are supposed to do—a mission, a plan, a design—and you really, deeply believe it, then you awake each morning with a sense of wonder and hopeful expectation. Could this be the day? What thing could happen to help me fulfill this special purpose? All of your life—even the bad parts—seem tied in to this wonderful possibility (when you really believe).

How can this be true in the midst of a world of convenience? Avoiding difficulty sells far better in the popular marketplace, than does adopting challenges. This brings into mind the words of The Master Teacher: *"Have faith and do not doubt, and you can say to this mountain, 'Go, throw yourself into the sea,' and it will be done"* (Mark 11:23).

What is meant by these mysterious words? We need challenges to take on. We need sizeable objectives to cause us to grow. We need to go after big mountains, to improve our "possibility thinking." We need gutsy projects to cause us to increase the horizons of our vision. The underlying message is: if we are faith believers, we will be mountain movers. So, let your goals be high enough that they "stretch" you, yet, real enough that you are really working on them, with faith!

Meditating on the encouragement of my friend Steve's words caused me to realize that my mountains were too small. As a result, I have re-challenged myself to have bigger goals, and to get busy trying to move bigger mountains.

This train of thought is all about motives and attitudes. If we do not break out of our limitations, then our limitations can break into us and cause us to be smaller than our potential promise. We should be known for our convictions of unlimited improvement, not as people imprisoned by our limitations.

Don't give in to the habit of our culture to get satisfied and complacent. Courageously face difficulty. Dare to "stretch" beyond what you have done before. Don't let your mountain be too small!

Action Required

Dare to move bigger mountains. What are things you suspect you can do but have been afraid to try? What does it matter if you fall short? You will still accomplish more trying to move your mountain than if you had not stretched for higher ground. Define some new "stretch" goals and go for them.

Phrases to Memorize

1. If we are faith believers we will be mountain movers.

2. *"My goals are high enough to "stretch" me and real enough that I am working on them daily, with faith!"*

MAKE TODAY GREAT

EXPONENTIAL IDEA 19

A Superball Success Strategy and Zanshin

Key Idea

Down is Not Always Bad

A seed must go down in the ground before it springs up into new life. Down can actually be a moment of rebirthing and re-energizing. The key is to look at it and treat it that way.

❧❧

It does not matter how far you have gone down. As long as you humbly (not arrogantly) ask God for help, you will get it. Furthermore, it has been my experience that He will probably bring you back up higher than before (like a superball). Additionally, to make sure that you get the message, He has put people in your path, like me, to help you see this truth.

A spring must be compressed before it expands with power. A rocket must be firmly situated on a ground platform, to ensure maximum take-off thrust. Human beings often must learn through some "down" experience, before they develop their wings and learn to fly.

In business, a crushing failure is often the catalyst needed to start a new track record of success. Likewise, in our personal lives, some habit or compulsion must often cause us pain before we see the light of freedom to overcome it. Down is not necessarily bad, if it leads to up.

Zanshin is a term used in all Japanese martial arts. It literally means "remaining mind." It is the body's posture after a technique is executed.

This moment is critical. The full explosion of energy must be naturally followed by a complete and heightened readiness—a state of emptiness of preconception that can react rapidly to anything; a state of natural preparedness that causes one technique to flow into the next.

It amazes me how perfectly a cat often embodies this state of readiness. Effortlessly and flawlessly, a cat can go from relaxed to engaged, from stealth to predator.

Just because you have experienced a "down" season does not mean you are powerless to win in your circumstances. Our capacity to win in our undertakings is often like a radio. The radio itself is neither good nor bad. Tuned into dirges and discordant sounds of mayhem, it can cause depression and melancholy. Yet tuned into bright and encouraging songs and messages, it can cause happiness and contentment. The key is the channel to which the radio is tuned.

We, like the radio, have control over our tuning. We can choose to tune into a critical, depressive way of thinking and expect a poor outcome for our work performance, or we can tune into an ambitious, confident thought channel and be assured of increased success.

There are myriads of people who have turned disadvantage into accomplishment. Thomas Edison, Abraham Lincoln, Colonel Sanders, Albert Einstein, Oprah Winfrey, Bill Gates and on and on the list could go. Despite horrible struggles, these people refused to stay down, took advantage of their opportunities, and proved the fact of the *Superball Success Strategy*.

Do not look at your failure and disappointment as the end. See it as a launching pad; a solid platform from which to explode; a bottom that you will leave and see only in your rear view mirror, as you move upward and forward to new vistas.

❧❧

Action Required

Change the channel on your poor outlook. Respond to your current situation with positive enthusiasm. Believe that you will see your achievements increase. Down isn't bad, as long as you don't stay there. Get up and win. Make the decision today to be like a superball and bounce higher than you have ever been before.

Phrases to Memorize

1. Down can actually be a moment of rebirthing and re-energizing.

2. As long as you humbly (not arrogantly) ask God for help, you will get it.

MAKE TODAY GREAT

EXPONENTIAL IDEA 20

The Peril of Limiting Beliefs

Key Idea

What We Believe About Ourselves Can Empower Us or Stop Us in Our Tracks

Replacing beliefs that hinder our progress with beliefs that encourage our progress is critical to growth and development.

❧❧

The importance of this lesson gripped me so strongly, that I discarded one of my already developed ideas to include this exponential thought. Limiting beliefs are the "arsenic" that poisons many people from achieving—who could and should succeed.

If we do not have a faith outlook, we are often doomed to demise only because of our own flawed belief system. The

Master Book of Wisdom says that *"Faith is the substance of things hoped for and the evidence of things not seen"* (Hebrews 11:1). In other words, faith is the *real stuff* that helps turn day dreams into visions and reality.

And the thing that stops most of us from having thoughts of faith that lead to better lives is fear, especially the fear of failure. It is amusing to watch a powerful 1,000 plus-pound bull veer away from a line, because he has been conditioned by the pain of an electric fence. The bull will still avoid this boundary even when it is cut off, because he fears the pain. Dogs who stay in the yard because of the collar shock of an underground line are exactly the same. And we are no different.

If we have been stopped by something repeatedly, we are fearful to try again. The pain of ridicule, discouragement, disappointment, and more are severe deterrents that keep us from trying again.

The worst part of limiting beliefs is that we most often do not know we have them. They are not external blocks we can see but internal blocks that can easily escape our attention.

Not only do our experiences cause us to have limitations in our confidence and outlook, but our culture and heritage does as well. Often, a good thing can become very limiting in this way. Some good value and truth that our forefathers have followed becomes a mandate in our minds, without our understanding the thought behind their practice. When we have imposed limits because of walls like this, without understanding the point of them, then these are entrenched obstacles and not positive traditions.

How do you know if you have internalized walls like this that are stopping you from growing? Usually, the answer to this becomes obvious when we honestly ask ourselves, *"Is the conviction faith-based or fear-based?"* Fear of retribution is not a conduit of positive change. Faith in principles you have thought through, is a stream of healthy growth and dynamic energy. Asking yourself, *"Is my belief fear-based or faith-based?"* and really experiencing the discovery about your motives, can turn a mindless fear that limits growth, into a mindful faith that causes meaningful action.

Self-worth statements can help you overcome internal limiting beliefs. I am not talking about wild-minded platitudes, where you unrealistically tell yourself you can reach the moon. I mean specific goal-oriented statements that address your limitations. For instance, maybe you have discovered you do not have a better exercise habit because of previous ridicule in this area. So a worth statement might be, *"I believe that I will succeed in developing a healthy exercise habit. I have confidence that I will achieve better conditioning. I am going to do this by . . . "* (and define your new approach). Look at yourself in the mirror and say this new belief statement daily, until you can make the image looking back believe it!

Oh! There is one really important thing to realize about these positive, self-worth statements; if you need to develop a new healthy statement, then that probably means you already have an unhealthy fear-based one running in the private theatre of your mind. So the really big key to making self-worth statements work is catching yourself when you are thinking the wrong thoughts, and replacing them with good ones.

Yes, experience can be a teacher. But you should remember that it can also be a thief. In what areas have your experiences caused you to believe you cannot win? These limiting beliefs— caused by misinterpreted experiences—are a great place to start in growing a new powerhouse of positive, goal-oriented, growth thinking. By this process of honest evaluation and replacement of flawed thoughts with healthy thoughts, you can actually turn your greatest liabilities into your greatest assets.

Consider these keys to remember as you work on replacing your limiting beliefs:

1. You are never through. Always be looking to grow with stronger, more empowering beliefs.

2. Believing that which strengthens and causes you to grow may require some discipline, but it will result in the freedom of a better life.

3. The best way to get outside yourself, and see limiting beliefs, is to value the advice of others. Stay humbly open to empowering suggestions.

4. Better advice cannot be given than: *"Seek and you will find"* (Matthew 7:7). Soul searching is the key. Have daily times of focus and meditation.

5. Honesty is also key. Denial is so easy to do and will keep you shallow and empty.

6. Get real with yourself. Sometimes growth requires some uncomfortable stretching to obtain.

7. Sabbaticals can change your life. Sometimes the only way to change is to stop everything and make a fresh start. Dare to do this, if you have tried other things and they have not worked.

❧❧

Action Required

What areas have your experiences caused you to believe that you cannot win? Identify these limiting beliefs. Develop positive faith convictions and confident outlooks to replace them with. Daily, work on replacing fear-based thinking with faith-based vision.

Phrases to Memorize

1. Limiting beliefs are the "arsenic" that poisons many people from achieving—who could and should succeed.

2. Faith is the *real stuff* that helps turn daydreams into visions and reality.

MAKE TODAY GREAT

EXPONENTIAL IDEA 21

Positive Connections—Be a Good Partner

Key Idea

Life is Not Meant to be Lived as an Island

We are designed to be in healthy relationship to others. The key word here is "healthy". Our connections either inspire us or deflate us. Learning to have constructive, positive interactions is an indispensable part of a life that grows in wellness, fulfillment, and purpose.

❧❧

Corporations need connections. They must have suppliers, accounting partners, shipping partners, service providers, and on and on the list can go. If there are no healthy connections, then there can be no healthy corporations.

Athletic teams must have good connections, and good interactions must be present with the coaches, players, fans, and financial supporters just to name a few, so the team can be successful.

Schools must have dynamic connections. They must relate well to their teachers, to their community, to their academic suppliers, to the parents and associated families, and especially, to the students.

Candidly, successful connections form the basis for every healthy organization on Earth, and they do the same for individuals. We all thrive best when our personal and professional connections are vital, supportive, and meaningful.

Connections are forms of touch, and extensions of interactions. Even in the ultimate sense of faith, connection is critical. My life has been a story of a faith connection with God. Not only has The Divine Spirit touched me, I believe He has changed the course of my life, and has allowed me to touch Him.

This connection is absolutely crucial to my health and well-being. Therefore, if you are looking for more wholeness in personal or professional dimensions, I suggest you start in this area. It has been my experience that spiritual connectedness will benefit, in many ways.

Still, regardless of your spiritual connectedness, the indisputable fact is that your interactions are likely to be the springboard to your overall success, or the cause of your failure.

In my professional past, I worked many years for a European furniture hardware company called Hafele. During the 80s and early 90s, the company published a newsletter for employees. They allowed me to write a section in the newsletter called "Positive Connections." I thought it was a "catchy" phrase for an inspirational column. So I wrote the column around this healthy thought title.

The underlying constructive idea I wrote about, was that healthy connections with God, our-selves, friends, and work lead to happier, more meaningful lives. Having only a few shallow connections will lead to meager meaning. Excellent and plentiful connections will lead to great meaning!

The key to getting something you can use from this evident fact, is being able to be honest about your own interactions. Ask yourself the following questions:

1. Do I have enough connections with others or would I benefit from more ties and relationships?

2. How do my current relationships affect me spiritually, psychologically, emotionally, intellectually and practically?

3. Am I a good person with which to connect? What can I do to improve my current connections?

4. Am I being truthful with myself about the state of my current connections? Where might I be derailing my progress by a lack of honesty with myself?

5. Do I give as much as I take? Do others value my personal and professional relationship because I give back? Or could my interactions improve, if I would invest more in them?

6. When is the last time I candidly assessed that the reason a connection is not developing is due to my own failure?

7. Am I willing to sacrifice selfish habits and tendencies, to grow my connections with others?

Answering these questions will help you strengthen and improve your ties to those who are important for you to connect with.

❧

Action Required

Am I a good partner? What can I do to improve the amount and quality of my connections? Identify some specific things to try right now and implement these changes as a definite target on your daily calendar.

Phrases to Memorize

1. Life is not meant to be lived as an island. We are designed to be in healthy relationship to others.

2. *"Am I willing to sacrifice selfish habits and tendencies, to grow my connections with others?"*

EXPONENTIAL IDEA 22

Positive Connections—Increase Your Appeal

Key Idea

We Can Increase Our Appeal to have More Positive Connections

Some topics cannot be overemphasized. The ideal of positive connections is one of those. So, if we believe that our positive connections will greatly increase the fulfillment of our life, then, how do we increase our appeal to have more positive connections?

❧❧

You already know the word "appeal" by one context for sure; our world is absolutely possessed and consumed by sex appeal. Nearly everyone wants to be more desirable to the other sex. This is certainly no secret. If one is able to market successfully this appeal, then people will beat his or her door down.

So if it is so powerful, what is sex appeal? That's simple. It is when you are desirable and people of the other sex want you.

Professional appeal is not such a raving topic, but if we approach it right, it should be. In the same way that certain things can make someone "appeal" to the other sex, there are certain things that can make a more personal and professional "appeal" to colleagues and work partners. This kind of appeal really is something you can take definite steps to increase and improve in your connections and relationships. Here are some solid suggestions:

1. Absolutely greet people warmly and with contagious friendliness. First impressions are crucial. The moments of first contact with someone can radically mold the environment of the dialogue—and move it—towards a great relationship. Whether you feel like it or not, greet people with warmth and friendliness. This is not phony . . . far from it. If you practice being enthusiastically friendly, you will become more genuine. It is a natural consequence.

2. Be outrageously positive. Sometimes when people ask me how I am, I will answer with a string of superlatives: amazing, awesome, dynamite, fantastic, incredible, blessed, happy, and energized. I can say a hundred more, at the drop of a hat. And I have practiced saying them so regularly that they spill from my tongue with energy and convincing persuasion. Nobody likes a dead fish. Be the kind of person who you would enjoy being around and you will find that others will like being around you!

3. Practice genuineness. The word "phony" is like an anathema for me. It is like a plague to be avoided at all costs. Being real with people will more often than not win them over to you. Nothing is more repelling to a connection than a non-genuine and insincere contact. To win connections and friends, let them sense that you are the real deal!

4. Be driven about value. I drive people in my organization crazy trying to serve customers well. It is not just a concept with me: it is a commitment. But that's where value must start. You are the face of your organization to others. Be driven about value! The word will get out and your positive career reputation will expand. People will seek you out, to join you.

5. Outlaw these: phony, negative, complaining, whining, disrespect, and resentment. People often wonder why they get poor results, when they have poor attitudes. Try to be real, positive, thankful, upbeat, respectful, and forgiving. If your attitude is good, you are much more likely to "appeal" to others.

6. Be passionate about success. Don't just "kinda, sorta" want to win. Passionately pursue excellence. Go after your best performance with zeal and gusto.

7. Learn to really care, not just put on an air. I try to have a prayerful attitude on the job. If someone has a need, I care. Do not just give lip-service to people. Practice being really interested in their welfare and it will greatly increase your "appeal."

8. Become an expert at what you do. People like to consult an authority. Do not just know enough to get by. Work on knowing enough to be an outstanding and expert connection.

9. Be comfortable in your own skin. Relax. Get loose. People are uncomfortable around uptight people. Enjoy what you do. Let your style shine, be the most poised person you can be. People will open up to you and tell you more if they sense you are contented with yourself.

10. Learn from others but develop your own style. It is a huge mistake to be unwilling to learn from others. It is also a huge mistake to be a copy-cat. Learn to have your own approach. Try the techniques of others but with your own style.

11. Develop the respect of your connections by being complimentary. If you bad talk those around you, people will not trust you. Work for and earn the respect of your connections. They will be more open to you as a professional, if they see that you are secure enough to recognize the talents and abilities of others.

12. Be humble and teachable. Yet, be strong and full of honest conviction. Be a person of balance who has a healthy view of others and yet a strong confidence in yourself. This will earn you the respect and admiration of others.

There are specific traits that will endear you to worthy strategic partners. Traits such as:

* Be a person who sees the value of connections. Learn to join things and put things together in your environment.

* Find ways not only to do better things but to do the things you already do, better. Strive to improve and function more efficiently and make it plain that this is your habit.

* Develop strategies to help other people and become known for this.

* Practice producing good things of benefit.

* Learn to add more value to the tasks you already do.

* Ensure the quality of your work. Let it be clear to all that know you that you are a person of high skill and competence.

* Be like Rosie the Riveter; put your name on what you do. This is not necessarily egotistical boasting. Just simply do good work and take honest credit for it.

ᔕᔐᔕ

Action Required

If you will practice these simple principles, you will definitely have healthier connections. People will love you and not even know why. I do not know that these principles will increase your "sex appeal," but they will definitely increase your personal and professional appeal. Write down some concrete ideas based on this chapter on how to increase your appeal to those of value, in your personal realm.

Phrases to Memorize

1. Be "outrageously positive."

2. *"I will develop strategies to help other people and become known for this."*

MAKE TODAY GREAT

EXPONENTIAL IDEA 23

Common Sense Solutions

Key Idea

***It is Easiest for People to Overlook that which is Widely
Known***

Common sense can often be taken for granted and therefore
missed altogether, because it is an assumed but neglected fact.
The following are some *"Check-up from the neck up"* (*Zigism)
tips we can all benefit from revisiting on a regular basis.

I penned these thoughts originally as sales solutions. Yet,
it has become plain that they are more than that; they are
great relationship guidelines in personal and professional
dimensions. Having an outstanding code for how you treat
other people can benefit you in every area.

❧❧

* Zig Ziglar was a positive thinking coach and motivational mentor.

119

Voltaire once said, *"Common sense is not so common,"* and in these simple words he drove home the point of this exponential idea. We need to continuously remind ourselves of the basics of communication and relationships. These commonly known facts are seldom practiced in the marketplace.

Point #1: Be Courteous

This seems so easy but is frequently so hard. This quality more than any other will qualify a sales organization for a brand of excellence.

Being nice to prospects and customers very frequently sets us apart from the other guys and makes them want to do business with us. I cannot count the times someone has told me they bought from me because they did not like the other guy, and I was nice to them.

Point #2: Put the Other Person First

Don't let your own policies be your failsafe. Let the interests of the person you are dealing with be your preferred position. The old "customer is always right" mindset is the greatest "common sense" failsafe to attract and keep valued partners in life and business.

"Common Sense Aint Common." **-Will Rogers

**Will Rogers was the most well-known spokesman for America in the 1920s and 30s, for wisdom and wit.

Point #3: Respond Quickly to the Requests of Others

In all high-ranking customer service businesses, this quality is always present. Whether it is answering the phone quickly or getting back to a prospect who wants information quickly. The point of treating your others with the high priority of helping right away can be a powerful catalyst to grow the relationship or close the sale.

Point #4: Practice a Habit of Restraint

Don't lose your cool; don't let a confrontational person lure you into a destructive trap. Controversy is never solved by turning up the heat. Turn it down a notch. Practice treating the person with respect, even if they do not do that with you. Just remember that you can always practice your own professionalism, in every context. Look at the histrionic customer as an opportunity to grow your own patience and posture. You cannot win if you blow up. Diffuse the situation by asking questions. Even if you have to correct the situation, do it with the minimum amount of conflict possible.

"Common Sense is seeing things as they are, and doing things as they ought to be." -Harriet Beecher Stowe

Point #5: Get Down to Business

Treat other people's time as a precious premium. Expedite your business with people. Get to the bottom line. Don't make your others feel that they cannot get a straight answer from you. Don't beat around the bush. Get to the bottom line. Let your contact extend the conversation if they want to, but personally be in a habit of streamlining and making your business with them more efficient.

Point #6: Go the Extra Mile (Matthew 5:41)

This is an incredible passage from the Good Book. It points out the powerful strength of doing more than is required. If you do the extra on a consistent basis, you will develop a reputation in the marketplace and the community for providing this kind of service. Your life and career will benefit if you consistently try to do a little extra for people than they expect from you.

"The only thing a person can never have too much of is common sense." -Kathryn Smith

Point #7: Find the Solution

People recommend people who provide them answers. Be a problem solver; make it a point to find answers for your customer's needs. When someone comes to you with a problem and you find an innovative way to help them, word gets around. Then, you will develop a healthy marketplace reputation as a problem solver.

Point #8: Put on Your Contact's Shoes

Empathize with the person you are dealing with and try to look at it from their point of view. Sales is about what they want, not what you want. Successful relationships are often the same. If others see that you genuinely want to help them out, you will win a high percent of the time. In fact, you both will (it is what Dr. Denis Waitly calls: *"The Win, Win"*).

"A sense of Humor is just common sense dancing."
-William James

Point # 9: Smile

"It's good for your face. It will brighten the place. It's easy to do. It's good for you" and others (The Hemphill's song, "I Can Smile," paraphrased).

Be genuine, real, and engaging . . . and sincerely smile.

Point # 10: Listen

It's not accidental that I saved this one for last. Salespeople often do not know that good listening is not passive; it is active. Get genuinely into what your others are telling you. Repeat what they say. Make sure you get it, because you are interested. Absolutely nothing is a more effective technique to strengthening relationships than listening with energy and interest.

"It is the obvious which is so difficult to see most of the time." -Isaac Asimov

Action Required

Remember these "Common Sense" relationship techniques. More important than that, practice them! Your personal life and professional life will improve if you do.

Ask yourself how you can get better at putting the other person first. Write down these ideas and carry them on a card in your purse or wallet and refer to them regularly. The point is that if you put others first, you will attract this kind of attention from them.

Phrase to Memorize

Having an outstanding code for how you treat other people can benefit you in every area of your life!

MAKE TODAY GREAT

EXPONENTIAL IDEA 24

Detra's Lessons—A Healthy Outlook

Key Idea

The Power of Acceptance, and Seeing Life as a Patchwork Quilt, are Two of Life's Greatest Lessons

My dear sister Detra passed away nine years ago, but the invaluable lessons she taught me never will. The power of acceptance and the healthy outlook of looking at life as a patchwork quilt, are two of these lessons. These principles have changed my life and have the power to change yours.

❧❧

I think about my deceased sister Detra, nearly every day. I lost her to cancer in 2005. She battled bravely but did not survive. She was my best friend. We shared, laughed, dreamed, cried, and worshipped together.

Sometimes (a lot of times actually), it takes greater courage to accept a thing than to fight it. I remember when my sister Detra was fighting cancer; she gave it all she had. As long as there was any chance of changing it, she fought with an amazing bravery. But when the cancer was in her internal organs, lungs and brain, it was plain that she was going to leave this earthly realm.

Until then, I had never seen anyone have such courageous acceptance. You would probably not know she was sick, until she was hospital confined at the very end.

She held her head high with dignity, found as much joy as she could in her final days and faced her fate bravely. She helped all those around her accept what she already had accepted.

I have learned from Detra's example. She had GUTS. She had a rare kind of courageous acceptance.

Some situations we have to deal with. They are not going away. The best way to cope with them is to accept them and go on. Acceptance! Think about that word. Life is easier to handle when we learn the peace of accepting the things we are going to have to deal with anyway.

I am not naturally good at accepting anything. I don't like to admit it but I usually feel that if I can fight hard enough or try with enough force, I can change anything (which is ridiculous, by the way).

I am only now learning in any real depth, the amazing power of the Serenity Prayer:

"Lord, grant me the serenity to accept the things I cannot change, the courage to change the things I can, and the wisdom to know the difference."

Another lesson, among the myriad of powerful lessons my sister Detra taught me, before she graduated from this realm, was the wisdom of comparing life to a patchwork quilt. It was one of the most gripping truths she ever shared with me. She painted in words the comparison of life with a patchwork quilt. On one side, a patchwork quilt is a series of tatters, unseemly seams and motley patterns. Yet on the other side of the quilt, there is a striking array of color, harmony, and lovely design, arrayed in intricate detail.

Life properly perceived is akin to a patchwork quilt. On one side, its disarrayed tatters, challenges, and problems, can seem like the whole of life is a bothersome sight. Yet life is only realized well, when the beautiful side is considered primarily.

When the color, the wonder, the design, the beauties, the attractiveness, and the goodness of life is looked at intensely. Life takes on its truest shade of meaning, dearness, and truth.

We would do well to concentrate on my sister's lesson in viewing our own lives. Only when dwelling on our blessings—the things of value and worth—can we attract more of the same and build the patchwork tapestry of our lives.

Concentrate on the bright side of your life. That is the best way to achieve the highest potential. Who knows? By thinking more about what you have to be thankful for than what you are concerned about, you may learn that life is more abundant with God's goodness than you realize.

One thing that prevents people from discovering and adopting their own exciting sense of mission, is that they cannot see how it will turn out. Good vision cannot always see the end of the path, but it can see the next step. Spiritual mission does not always mean you see the whole picture, but that you have enough faith to make the next stroke of your brush mean something. We should not be afraid to take the next stroke just because we cannot see how the work will turn out.

If we see this spiritual mission as the grand work of art God means for us to see it as, we will aim to paint our most beautiful creation with the brush-strokes of life. My sister Detra was the greatest artist I have ever seen. Yet, in comparison to the greatness of her work, she was not greatly known. Even still, her work grandly changed me, and her daring heart—ever willing to design, create, and invent—was indomitable. Your greatest dream should be to be all you can possibly be, and if it is a good dream, you will translate it into action . . . like Detra did. In the end of life, it may be all that matters.

My precious sister Detra, smiling as she fought a fatal bout with cancer.

I remember that in Detra's demise in her fight with cancer, she held her head regally high. She demonstrated to me her sense of spiritual mission, even in the end of life. Courage does not always know if it is going to win, but if it believes the cause is worthy and the timing right, it fights anyway. She proved this to me and I intend to keep the heart of her lesson, in my own life.

❧

Action Required

1. Live daily in the lessons taught by the Serenity Prayer. Learn to have the peace to accept what you cannot change and the courage to change what you can.

2. Make a decision to look at your existence in its most healthy terms, and you will discover more beauty and meaning in your life.

Phrase to Memorize

When the color, the wonder, the design, the beauties, the attractiveness, and the goodness of life are looked at intensely, life takes on its truest meaning.

༄ In Loving Honor of Detra Carol Carter ༉

MAKE TODAY GREAT

EXPONENTIAL IDEA 25

Workplace Satisfaction—10 Keys

Key Idea

Gaining Satisfaction from Your Career Adds to a Happier, More Enriched Life

Part of the fascination I have in addressing the workplace as a primary topic, is a feeling that this task is congruent with my background of ministry. Since we spend a large portion of our lives working, one clear way I can be a benefit to you is by adding fulfillment to your professional life. If I can help you be happier in your career, then I have helped you to enrich your life. This assignment is actually an extension of what I see as my ministry to help others. So helping you get more satisfaction out of your career is linked to my own fulfillment.

❧❧❧

Being fulfilled in your work and being successful at doing it are hand in glove propositions; being effective at one contributes to the other. Who will do their best job if they do not gain satisfaction from their work? No one! It's like asking someone to climb Mount Everest when they don't like the mountains. It's not going to work. If you are a swimmer who is mountain climbing, that won't work. If you are mountain climber who is swimming, that won't work either.

Sometimes, what we are doing is not a fit for our skill-set or personality. If that's the case, quit trying to put a square peg in a round hole and find something that "fits" your talents, abilities, and interests better.

However, most times it is not a job repositioning, we need. If we don't address the difficulties that hold us back and haunt us in our current situation, we are not likely to overcome them in a new situation.

It's a funny picture of the cow overlooking his own grassy meadow, trying to reach the single blade of grass on the other side of the fence. While it may be a funny picture, all too often, it is a sad reality. Some people never find fulfillment because they are always looking for it somewhere else. Fulfillment is most often found where we are today. And then when we move elsewhere—because we outgrow and master the current situation—we see our next steps and more will be revealed to us.

If we run from problems in our current situation, we will likely find them in different faces and different places, only bigger than before.

So, assuming you are in a healthy career situation for you, following are some great helps to get more satisfaction out of your workplace.

Workplace Satisfaction Key #1

Never forget that the soul is a channel you can control. Happiness is to a great degree a simple matter of choice. If you decide you will be happy, you will be. Go to work with a good attitude and you greatly increase your chances of liking your workplace. Make up your mind before you go in the door that you will make the best of the day. This may not be clever originality, but it is critical to adding more satisfaction to your job.

Workplace Satisfaction Key #2

Belief is the x factor. Believe in yourself. Believe in the positive aspects of what you do. And believe in your own ability to achieve. These are karma components. To hit the target, you must aim for the bull's-eye. Work on empowering beliefs. Work on the inner dialogue that nobody hears but you. Begin to say positive affirmations to yourself, about your direction. Far from being hype, this is the rocket fuel to blast you in the right direction.

Workplace Satisfaction Key #3

Put a few things on your desk and your work area that make you smile. And change this up every once in a while. Evaluate these personal brighteners by their ability to encourage. Don't daydream about them but have them there for that moment when you need a personal power boost.

Workplace Satisfaction Key #4

Change up your schedule with mood lifters. Schedule a lunch with a friend or a child. Bring a photo to a meeting that makes everybody laugh. Find a good joke hotline or daily email and share it with someone else. Moments of mirth, though brief, can add just enough levity to make you happier and your workday more productive.

Workplace Satisfaction Key #5

Remember the power of purpose. Design as many of your workplace activities as possible. Nothing is more frustrating than letting your day drift, without a sense of purpose. Keep a good aim on projects that benefit the company and encourage you at the same time. As mentioned, Dr. Denis Waitley called this *"The win, win."* Certainly you will have to do things you don't like, but you can balance these by cheerfully developing things you do like. Your employer may not go for all your ideas but should appreciate that you are thinking and want to add personal value to the business.

Workplace Satisfaction Key #6

Remember that boredom is never fun. Challenge yourself. We are happiest when working in the highest realms of our good. Even failures feel good, when they are part of healthy and constructive ambition. Don't try foolish tasks; use common sense. But dare to take on that which is challenging. Your colleagues and superiors will appreciate your initiative, and you will find happiness in your own productivity.

Workplace Satisfaction Key #7

Be pleasant to others. Nobody likes a jerk. What have you done recently to be courteous to someone new? Be good to people. Make it a point to be friendly. As a general rule, if you are friendly with people, they will be friendly with you. Grab a doughnut for a workmate, or if they are health-conscious, a granola bar. The point is to enjoy your associates in the workplace. If you do this, you will find that when you least expect it, they will return the favor to you.

Workplace Satisfaction Key #8

Remember that time is always short. You can't relive a single day. Identify things that seem gratifying at the moment—like web surfing—that seem rewarding but detract from the bigger picture of your daily achievement. Make each day count by making the most of each moment.

Workplace Satisfaction Key #9

Remember that resentments in the workplace do not hurt the person you resent, as much as they hurt you. Keep your heart and mind free of the clutter of this unnecessary debris. Think good thoughts about even those you do not like. This way, you will keep them from living rent free in your head. Do not let frustrating thoughts run you. Keep your mind clear by keeping your heart on a higher path. You can accomplish more in your work arena if you do not let conflicts with workmates take up space in your head.

Workplace Satisfaction Key #10

Keep who you are at a higher premium than what you do. Let your work life be an extension of your beliefs and values. Find ways to have a meaningful view of everything. Let your home motivate your work and let your work add value to your home. Live in a bigger picture than the clutter of the moment. Do the next right thing always and believe that you are painting a masterpiece, even when all you can see is the single stroke of the paintbrush of your current moment.

❧❧

Action Required

Always give more than you take. Do not worry about giving out. There is a providential plan in place that guarantees givers will always have more to give. *"Give, and you will receive. Your gift will return to you in full, pressed down, shaken together, to make room for more, running over, and poured into your lap. The amount you give will determine the amount you get back."* -Jesus

Phrases to Memorize

1. If we don't address the difficulties that hold us back and haunt us in our current situation, we are not likely to overcome them in a new situation.

2. Fulfillment is most often found where we are, and then it grows into something more, somewhere else, because we outgrow the situation we've mastered.

MAKE TODAY GREAT

EXPONENTIAL IDEA 26

Energy in the Office

Key Idea

Everyone in the Business Realm has to Work Some in the Office

If you can add more vitality and energy into the office, then it has an overall positive effect not only your work, but also your work enjoyment.

❧❧

For most of my career, I traveled all around the South, Southeast, continental US, and even abroad. Having energy for a life of travel is a far different topic than the office (maybe in my next book, I will cover it).

Many of you find yourself in an office setting, day after day. These thoughts are particularly aimed at helping you with your time in the office.

I started in an office setting many years ago and then grew into outside sales and sales management. Some changes were necessary, and these changes led me back into the office setting. What a shocker it was to land back in an office, at the end of my employment career.

I found it difficult to come back into the office environment to work again. Therefore, I taught myself techniques to improve my own happiness and energy flow in the office. Some may seem obvious, yet the obvious is the hardest to achieve for many. We know it, but don't do it. So don't gloss over the obvious. It may be the missing piece of the puzzle you need.

I also discovered things not quite so obvious to improve mental hygiene and work attitude in the office. These require a little work. All of these will improve the way you work and feel in the office:

1. Get adequate rest the night before. This seems so obvious, but it is frequently a culprit when we don't feel good at work. Want to feel better in the office? Get enough sleep at home.

2. Take walks on your breaks. To feel better at the desk, take active breaks from the desk. Don't spend them all at the coffee pot. Even if you only have time to cruise around the parking lot, the stretching and stimulation will get your blood flowing and change your mental outlook.

3. Put on smiles when no one is looking. Put a big ole grin on your face. I'm not talking about just when you feel like it but also when you don't. Literally stretch your facial muscles and slap a huge beaming smile on your face. It's strange, but it will make you feel better. And if you get caught, so what, it will keep your workmates guessing.

4. Stand up when talking on the telephone. This is huge. This is not original with me, but it was revolutionary to me, when I quit reading about it and started trying it. Try it. Your erect body posture will, a) make you sound better to your customers, b) change the pace in your office, c) force you to think about what you say, and d) increase the calories you burn in a day. Try it!

5. Do isometrics at your desk. Look up the word. You can pull one hand against the other, push your palms together, exert force against your table top, stretch and move your neck around, massage your hands. There are literally limitless exercises you can do right at your own desk that won't take you away from your work, but will make you feel better doing it.

6. Be careful about sugars, especially in your coffee. Loading up your coffee with sugar may give you energy, but it will often result in an unpleasant crash of your energy resulting from hypoglycemia.

7. Drink lots of water. I don't mean sip it. Drink it . . . a lot of it. Regularly count your fluid ounces. Keep your body hydrated to feel better through the day.

8. Watch the heavy meals; comfort foods are just not comforting when they make you want to fall asleep at your desk. Don't overeat if you want to stay alert. Be reasonable and don't fill up with a lot of greasy, heavy, foods.

9. Fun is fun. Keep a healthy, tasteful joke running with your colleagues. Loosen up and enjoy your workmates. A little laughter in the office will make the day go better. Bring a joke to work sometimes. Look for the good in those around you. You cannot work in close proximity with others and be happy, unless you do your part to make the work environment pleasant.

10. Utilize diversion tools. What do I mean? The Staples "easy button" is a great example. You press the button and it rewards you with encouragement to lighten up. I used to put rocks on my desk that I enjoyed picking up. I changed it up and put Chinese work out balls on my desk to twirl around in my fingers. Things that do not take away from productivity but increase activity and maximize your attention level are the kinds of tools you need for this.

11. Wash your face . . . literally. The Bible teaches that when you fast, do not let others know you are fasting, and one of the ways it tells you to avoid others knowing is to wash your face. Wash your face and feel better. Wash your face and look better. Wash your face and your outlook changes. Don't forget to use this as an energy boosting tool at work.

12. I have a friend who drives me crazy with Feng Shui. But I have discovered that he is right. There is a way to organize things that works, and ways that don't.

13. A like topic—but not the same—is ergonomics and synergistic techniques. Changing one little thing about your work environment can literally change your health, improve your circulation, and avoid carpal tunnel. Read up on this. Get suggestions from friends. Rearrange your office space to improve ergonomics.

14. Arrange active social breaks weekly. Meet your mother, brother, sister, friend, minister etc. for lunch. Keep some variety in your schedule and your work-week.

15. Ruts are not schedules. If something does not feel right, it may not be right. If something does not seem to work about your work, change it if you can. Tell your employer that you are working on ways to increase efficiency. When they understand you are trying to improve work performance, employers will often work with you on this.

16. Stand in meetings. Meetings can be killers to mental alertness. When possible, I stand in the back of the room at meetings. Usually, people will know you are trying to be more attentive, and appreciate it.

17. Change your chair. A crappy chair makes you feel crappy. Invest in your own posture and comfort. Work from a decent chair.

18. Give yourself visual pleasures. Put tasteful pictures in your office, if allowed. Put a sculpture on your desk. Have something pleasant to look at, to lift your mood as you work.

19. Last but not least. Watch the sauce the night before. You cannot feel good or work well in the office if you are hung over.

⋐⋑⋐⋑

Action Required

When a car is not running good, you work on it until it runs better. It's the same with your office environment. Try these suggestions to get more work out of your day, and enjoyment out of your work. If you work on them, I guarantee you more energy in your office.

Phrase to Memorize

"There are things I can do to improve my own happiness and energy flow in my office."

MAKE TODAY GREAT

EXPONENTIAL IDEA 27

Get Your Eyes off the Stack, and Attack

Key Idea

Many Great Accomplishments in Life Happen, When we Turn a Notion into Motion

Work can become like a stack of unresolved paperwork. It daunts us with challenge. As long as we just look at it, the challenge only seems to increase. Yet, when we dig into the stack with determination and ferocity, we find that which intimidated us is not so daunting after all. Triumph over adversity is wonderful and can be commonplace, when we adopt this kind of winning approach. Often, the answer to work stress is to take our eyes off the stack, and attack!

❧❧

143

In the sales dimension, winning is frequently as simple as refusing to be beaten. Having a dogged, determination that sees problems as expected hurdles and not impossible walls, can change everything about your performance.

Let this exponential idea fuel the fire of your determination. The best way to lose is *not* to try. Not asking the question fails to get an answer, every time. The best way to get a *"No"* is to fail to ask. Victory awaits only those with the will to win. Get your eyes off the stack, and attack!

What do you do when you don't know what to do? Not knowing what to do can prevent people from doing anything. It can lure them into being overwhelmed, uncertain, indecisive, procrastinating, inefficient, discontent, and a having a lack of vision. So, let's look at a simple habit that can help in all these areas.

As a Quaker, I like simplicity. I center on the clear direction of my Creator always being available. This is a simple and clear way to live. The goal of saying this is to point out the power of simplicity.

We live in a world that complicates everything. Tedious tasks and difficult duties fill our lives. In every realm—and particularly the business realm—this can be lethal! If problems and details overwhelm direction and energy, an overload can occur . . . an overload that leaves us in such a state, that we don't know what to do. I have found the answer to this uncertainty is a simple philosophy: *do the next right thing!*

The Answer to an Overwhelming Workload

A common ailment of our world is people wanting more for less, from us. If you are a person of initiative and accept these terms, people who recognize this will take advantage of you. They will see just how full they can fill your plate. So it is easy

144

to find ourselves in situations where there is more to do than can possibly be done.

Of course the popular answer is to prioritize. That can be fine and useful, but sometimes it results in just reorganizing stacks of uncompleted work, and does not actually get anything done. In these overload situations . . . in these moments of perplexity, I have found simplicity is the answer.

I may not see the whole picture at times but I always can see the next right thing. It is like an internal guiding compass.

If we get our eyes off the stack, and attack the next *right* issue, an amazing thing happens. The stack gets smaller and we get more done. Therefore, do not focus on the stack, focus on the next right thing. When in an overwhelming situation, remember, the only way to eat an elephant . . . yep, that's right: one bite at a time. Take the next bite.

The Answer to Uncertainty

Sometimes not knowing what to do will cause people to not do anything, and this only causes the uncertainty to increase. Take action when facing a heavy load, even if it's a little action.

Everywhere I look people are saying *"Take massive action."* Wow! What's that? Am I supposed to go pick a fight with King Kong and expect to win? That kind of effort is not only *not* massive action, it is massive stupidity!

Generally, the way to take effective action is by taking a definite, little action, then taking another little action, then another and so on, until you discover that your productivity made a real difference. Then, with gratitude, you can look at the work completed and it will look massive compared to what would have been done, had you remained in the inaction of uncertainty.

The Answer to Indecision

Choices. Choices. Choices. Our society loves choices. Thus, what I say now may be unpopular, but sometimes there are just *too many* choices. You can get stuck analyzing choices and not *do* anything. Do not be lured into this trap.

In the Biblical account of Abraham and his nephew Lot, they were to part company. Abraham simplified the scenario. *"You go left and I will go right. You go right and I will go left."* He eliminated a choice! He knew whichever direction he went, God would go with him and bless him. So he let his nephew make the choice. Do not sweat the small stuff. Do not calculate every decision. Do what you believe is right and move on, and trust the results to providence.

The Answer to Procrastination

Boy! This is a tough one. How do I get you off your lethargic buttocks and make you do something? (*That* didn't win me any friends.)

I teach karate. And sometimes, I know a student is not giving me their best. Many times, I will get right behind him/her with a stick (literally) till they get the point and catch fire. It is easier to perform than have Sensei chase you with a stick . . . but really!

Sometimes we need to be stirred out of our complacency. Direct your foot appropriately, and correctly apply it to your own posterior. Remember, doing the next right thing starts with a two letter word: DO!

The Answer to Maximized Efficiency

I am fifty-five. I know I have less time in front of me than I do behind me. How do I achieve more with less time? The answer: do the right thing, do it right now, and do it again as often as I can, with as much intensity as I can.

The Answer to Personal Satisfaction

* The conscience strengthens with good conduct.
* The will resolves more firmly with good decisions.
* Personality harmonizes with healthy attitudes.
* Work streamlines with positive actions.

What is Right, right now? That is the imperative question. Answer it and act decisively. Make this kind of behavior a lifestyle, and you will find the rewards of greater happiness and satisfaction. They will become the trademarks of your life and career.

The Answer to New Vision

Where do we go from here? That seems to be the question on everyone's mind. Do not overlook today, to determine your future. It is in true service to God, our families, and our fellow man today, that we will find our brightest path for tomorrow.

All my life, I have had powerful instincts and hunches. I seem to possess a sixth sense about things, beyond the scope of reason or understanding. Yet, no extra senses are required to harness the intuitive power of effective living.

We each have inside us a compass—an inward sense of direction. It is a deep knowing of what to do and how to do it.

Eastern philosophies look at this as an inward flame. Some call it "ki strength." But whatever the nametag, there is definitely a deeper power source for life than what appears on the surface.

Be sold out doing the right thing today. Do it with all your heart and might. Call it karma. Call it law of the harvest. Call it what you will, but if you do the next right thing continually, you will find your life and career blessed with more abundance and an abiding, inward sense of direction!

❧❧

Action Required

Some things bear repeating for emphasis: how do I achieve more with less time? Do the right thing, do it right now, and do it again as often as I can, with as much intensity as I can.

Phrases to Memorize

1. Get your eyes off the stack, and attack.

2. Do the next right thing.

MAKE TODAY GREAT

EXPONENTIAL IDEA 28

Purpose Checkpoints

Key Idea

Checkpoints of Purpose Can Keep Us on Target

When law enforcement officers want to make sure that citizens are keeping current traffic related laws, they often set up checkpoints to ensure civil compliance. When we want to make sure we are on track with our lives, checkpoints of purpose can keep us on target.

❧❧❧

Some of this exponential thought dovetails with previous contents. A dovetail is a method of wood joinery, where one piece is joined to another through a joint that combines them. The point of this combination is to make something come together, that otherwise would not exist without joining the pieces.

As mentioned earlier in this book, we should reinforce the good changes we have developed in our life with positive gratification. We should mark the moment . . . celebrate the victory of our improvement. It is that *"Yahoo"* moment of driving through a police checkpoint, being glad you are okay and can continue on your way.

Also as mentioned, a good example of a purpose checkpoint is where we mark special events in our lives with an altar. Confirming what we have already learned keeps us from having to learn the same lesson twice. Something else, achieved by regular looks at the milestones in our lives, is practically staying on track with our goals.

A good example of one such purpose checkpoint is the practice of New Year's Resolutions. I recommend this but not only for the purpose of setting new goals. An equally important aim for this practical practice is evaluating how we did with the previous year's targets. What have you already purposed? How are you doing with it? How can this goal be refined or improved? A great benefit of this annual targeting is having the answers to these important questions.

Goal statements—like road checkpoints—have the value of being measures of accountability. When recorded and reviewed, they become progress indicators. They give us a very clear picture of how we are following through with our decisions for growth.

As I said, when I was a little boy, my mother took a yard stick and made marks on the closet door to show me how I was growing. Goal statements are similar to this practice. They show us how we are growing and give us a chance to measure up. They are a way to remind ourselves of what is really important. They are a way to get encouragement from our progress. They are great personal accountability tools.

Where are your goal statements? Can you put your hand on them? Whether you use Post-it Notes in prominent places, a daily planner, vision board, online journal or calendar, it cannot be stressed enough to have them.

I created the following acrostic to illustrate the importance of "working" goal statements:

G is for *Game Planning*
O is for *Our*
A is for *Active*
L is for *Learning*

Goals should not only be lofty ideals for which we stretch, but more than that, they should be practical tools we use to design and chart the purposefulness of our lives. They should be ongoing, learning instruments.

Even failed goals can be valuable when they are realized, examined, and utilized as learning tools. Which of your goals have you missed? Why? What did you learn from this purpose checkpoint, that you can do better in the future?

Marry your goal statements with regular points of review. Every smart journey is started with a map or directions . . . directions which should be consulted along the course of the trip. Your life should be like a targeted journey. It should be a charted trip that you compare to the map of your plans as you travel. Doing this will make your life have purpose and not just happenstance.

❧❧

Action Required

Whether you need to learn new lessons or revitalize concepts you have already realized, regular *Purpose Checkpoints* can help you achieve. Plan now how you will review your progress in the coming year. Marry your goal statements with regular points of review. Every smart journey is started with directions. Consult your map along the course of the trip, to ensure the success of your trip.

Phrase to Memorize

When we want to make sure we are on track with our lives, checkpoints of purpose can keep us on target.

MAKE TODAY GREAT

EXPONENTIAL IDEA 29

Compelling Vision—A Goal in Mind

Key Idea

Goals Combined with Initiative Produce Real Change

Goals must be combined with initiative to create real change, and this kind of approach to life and business produces a compelling vision. An approach like this is so strong that it is nearly unstoppable!

❧❧

Goals and Initiative

In 2004, when I remarried, my wife and I took on quite an undertaking. I had two children (a boy and a girl), and she had four boys. So, as we planned our new life together, we had to buy a house large enough to be a gymnasium. I had two and she had four; together, we had a mess!

As a good father, I have always tried to be kind to my own kids. Likewise, I was determined to adopt Dawn's boys as my own. Coming into this picture was complicated, since it was important to me to try to meet each of their individual needs. On this note, one of my first "goals" was to get the two youngest boys a goal: a basketball goal that is. It seemed like a great family project for us all to enjoy. It was a great idea, right?

It didn't work out that way. The boys rarely waited for my wife and me to move our cars. They played ball with the cars in the drive-way, even after being threatened with bodily harm. The balls were always hitting our cars, and they refused to change.

Furthermore, they refused to pick up the balls; they left them laying everywhere. Since *they* would not change, one day *I* did. I had enough of this irresponsibility, and I solved the problem. I threw the goal in the woods and got rid of all the balls. Balls always seemed to bounce back into our picture but the basketball goal never did. And there it sat for seven years, in our woods . . . seven long years. Seven years that caused it to deteriorate, crack and come apart. It literally became useless and existed only as an eyesore.

As part of a home fix-up project, I rescued the backboard from the woods. I fished it from its place of abandonment and thought I would repair it. Since the boys are now young men and hopefully more responsible, it seemed only natural to me to rescue it so they could play with it when they are here. But my wife, Dawn, quickly nixed that idea and made me take it to the road to sell it. She did not want to see it anymore and made me promise—unhappily—to get rid of it.

This did not solve the goal problem though. No one would buy it. So we took the *"For Sale"* sign off of it, and left it there to be hauled off by the city. It became plain that they didn't want it either. No one would pick it up . . . couldn't sell it, couldn't give it away, and couldn't trash it without a truck. What was I to do with the goal?

So I returned to my idea to fix it and salvage it. No one would believe that I could repair it. It reminded me of many of us, as we age and decline. That thought emboldened me all the more, to bring it back to life. No one else could see it but me; but I could see a new goal.

As I started my project, even in the shape it was in, my son Matt would prop it up and play with it. This convinced me even further that it had to be salvaged. The work ensued with a passion—a work that was made more difficult by my wife's firm resistance. We had to haggle about how it would look, what it would do to a garden, where we would put it, and how I would stop the balls from winding up in the woods. And she especially challenged me about whether I could really fix it.

Anyway, I became quite committed to completing the project, through this process of negotiating with my wife. I had a new goal in mind and my vision got clearer each time I had to sell her on it.

It didn't help my case much when I nearly broke my foot when I dropped the rebuilt, refortified backboard on it. At this point, my daughter started commenting about my obvious insanity. The news was conveyed to me in no uncertain terms; the women of the home did not want it just standing there on its own stand any more. They made it quite difficult to proceed. Still, this did not deter me. You see, I had a goal in mind.

So, the plan was born to make a concrete pad and then permanently place the redeemed backboard in the only spot the people in my family could envision it. There was a lot of work to be done, that no one but me believed I could do:

* Repair the cracks by building a new backboard base.

* Devise a way to re-secure the rebuilt backboard to the post, since all the anchors were broken and now would not fit.

* Find a separate way to reattach the goal, since it had long since come loose from the back board.

* Find a way to make sure the crooked frame would stand straight enough to allow play.

* Make sure the whole thing was sturdy enough for a ball to be blasted against it, and to have young men grabbing the goal.

156

Even though there were no pat-on-the-backs, I completed this project and played basketball on the mostly completed goal, with my stepson, and verified in my own mind that if I finished it, it would work. The goal loomed even larger in my mind.

Do you think new cracks created by people messing with it caused me to stop the work? In a word, NO! Frustrated, but not dismayed, I fixed them and began the cosmetic restore of the backboard. Here it is nearing completion.

And what is the point of all this? No one else believed I could salvage and make a workable piece of equipment out of the bits and pieces I had to work with. No one else believed it could be done. *But I did.* I had a goal in mind!

So, after finishing the tedious process of rebuilding the backboard, re-securing the backboard to the post, and then re-securing the goal to the post, I learned that the frame itself would not hold because of the weakness of the platform, which could not hold water or stand on its on. By this point, you may be sure *that* didn't deter me! My next steps were to prepare the ground and build a concrete and rock pad for it to sit on. The goal was in sight and this unexpected step didn't even faze me.

I built the concrete and rock base, and set the revitalized goal in place. And I was rewarded with the joy of watching my stepson play on it. My vision was turned into a reality. My goal is now in my driveway.

Perhaps you have similar situations in your life, where you would like to move forward but, a) no one else sees your vision, and b) no one else believes you can do it. That's okay! If it's a good goal, you can a) help them see your vision, and b) prove to them that you can do it. Just keep your goal in mind and do the work.

My good friend, Steve Gutzler, is an expert at helping people get more out of their lives and careers. He has helped me see that bigger marketplace goals still make sense for me. So what is the message for you, here?

* Great ideas can still be born, when all you have is broken pieces to begin with.

* Sometimes the only person who can see your vision at first is you, and this is okay.

* It may hurt some, to make your vision a reality. This is just part of the chance you take.

* You can "sell" others on your vision, a) if it is a good one, b) if you make positive progress, and c) if you will not give up.

* There will be bumps along the way. You may even have to scratch one plan and try another, but your vision will succeed if you believe and keep taking the next right steps.

As I wrap this up, the obvious message is, you will be sure to get there if you have a goal in mind and not stop until it's done.

❧❧

Action Required

Have your own compelling vision. If you do not have one, find one, and discover the steps you must take to bring your vision to reality. A personal, compelling vision of initiative, based on your goals, will help you succeed in a big way.

Phrase to Memorize

"I can be sure I will succeed if I have a goal in mind, and will not stop until it is done." (Say it repeatedly.)

MAKE TODAY GREAT

EXPONENTIAL IDEA 30

Have a Daily Focus Time

Key Idea

A Daily Focus Time Will Get You Where You Want to Go

Each day that you get up to go to work, you must start your car. If you forget to start it, it will not go. If we are to live effective, on-target lives, our operation is similar to our cars; we must start and maintain the functioning of our life for it to get us where we want to go. A *Daily Focus Time* can help you achieve more and be happier.

❧❧❧

Up to this point in this book you have read the following words:

Work, at least 139 times

Career, at least 45 times

Vision, at least 29 times

Purpose, at least 31 times

Faith, at least 24 times

Focus, at least 20 times

Courage, at least 10 times

Business, at least 25 times

Professional, at least 22 times

Meaning, at least 10 times

Energy, at least 25 times

Satisfaction, at least 30 times

Action, at least 33 times

Obviously this book has been greatly aimed to help you get more out of your work and career. It is directed to increase your vision, purpose, faith, focus, courage, business, professionalism, meaning, energy, and satisfaction in the workplace. These things are empowered by strategies to get you to "act" on what you have learned.

In that light, perhaps I have saved the best for last. There is little I can do to help you get more gratification out of your life, than cause you to have a *Daily Focus Time*.

There is joy and meaning to be found each and every day. Cheerfulness is a disposition, not a magic activity. Simple pleasures of music, flowers, sea, sky, animals, friends, and family can be enjoyed every day. There is joy in a cup of coffee. There is the happiness of a good meal, the mirth of a good joke, and the sense of satisfaction of a job well done. These and one million other delights can invade our senses each day, when we give them proper attention. We can experience these joys daily when our mind and heart are alive and open enough to appreciate them.

The problem that prevents many from having this kind of a healthy outlook is the lack of a definite approach in working on the task. To jumpstart my daily living, I literally have a time each day when the matters of my own soul and well-being are my one-hundred percent concern.

Daily joy can be lost when there is no concentrated effort to make it a priority. In the requirements and duties of each day, there is meaning and good. But this realization is a mindset that must be cultivated regularly.

Find and celebrate the blessings of each day. God's love and care are present, every day, including today. But, like any treasure, you must look to find it. I start and end each day with a definite time of focus, reflection, meditation, reading, and prayer.

Your focus time does not have to be just like mine to work. Yet, it must be daily and targeted to be effective. You can and should integrate thoughts of family, health, career, church, community, and service into the mix of this daily habit.

I cannot overstress to you how these times of empowerment, learning, and growth are as critical as fuel is to your car. You must be steady, relentless, and consistent to see the good of this enriching practice.

Be relevant, right now. Make a contribution today. The best time to feel good about your own efforts is when you are doing something good. Target your current efforts. Yesterday's aim will not do. You must aim again today. Let your *Daily Focus Time* be a time when you take good aim on today's tasks.

Be flexible. Roll with the punches. What you are doing today may not necessarily be what you do tomorrow. I recommend that you think a lot about the Serenity Prayer in your *Daily Focus Times*. You can shock people with your adaptability. By having a more accepting tolerance about things that you cannot change, you will greatly enhance your peace of mind and serenity.

Concentrate all of your intensity on the absolute ideal of what you want to achieve in these *Daily Focus Times*. Identify weaknesses and work on them. Identify strengths and focus on them. This will help you hit the bull's-eye. Even if you miss the bull's-eye, you will still hit the target strongly. Furthermore, these daily times of direction will help you make sure you clearly see the target in the first place.

For me, what I do to help others attain more satisfaction in the workplace is through service to God. I dedicate every day to Him, especially in my *Daily Focus Times*. I find this to be the surest ingredient to give daily balance to this walk of life.

❧

Action Required

Have a definite, purposeful time each day, when your own growth, development, and well-being are your complete focus during that time.

Phrase to Memorize

A *Daily Focus Time* can help you achieve more and be happier.

POSTSCRIPT

It has occurred to me that a book with the title, *Positive²
(positive x positive)=Unlimited*, would be incomplete without
a statement from the author about his power source. This
postscript will tell you where I get my power from.

I have experienced God to be the Master of the second
chance. Do not live in a flawed past; He will help you make
today new, and tomorrow better!

Spiritual refreshment does not come from without. It comes
from within, in the same way that a light bulb's power starts on
the inside first.

Standing underneath a waterfall is always exhilarating.
A genuine relationship with God is like that! There is always
something powerful going on inside!

If you want people to see a better you on the outside, let your
Maker create a new you on the inside.

The clean water that one drinks from a spring always comes
from a pure source. Get plugged in to the right power source for
a cleaner life!

Life growth should be like contents under pressure. Let so
many good things happen on the inside, and you cannot help
but let them bubble out!

We restrict God because of our lack of comprehension. He
wants to build something more wonderful on the inside of us
than we can understand.

Do not restrict God by your mental box . . . He is beyond
anything you can imagine. To experience Him, you must allow
yourself to grow beyond that.

God's Spirit can be like a mega super-charged refreshing flood inside; you cannot explain it but you can experience it with an open heart!

A humble and contrite spirit that knows how small you are in the light of the Divine Majesty, and a yielded mind, makes the vessel of your heart ready.

Love for God should be like an electric explosion on the inside of you, as you rejoice and worship the Divine Maker who is so real and true.

If your mind, will, and purpose is to cause God joy with your life, He will open mysteries to you and reveal His beautiful plan, if you seek Him.

Often, God does not allow me to share all He shows me. Some of it is like a private and powerful song in my heart just for me. He will do the same for you.

To be affiliated with a cleansing fire, one must not grieve that personal impurities are burned away. The relationship is worth the price! Grace, mercy, kindness, strength, honor, compassion, courage, love, and wisdom can exist inside you, if you yield to Him who IS all these things.

Sometimes God opens a faucet of expression and lets me share joys of His beauty with others. He wants to use us, in His time, as His vessels.

Be blessed today my friends. You are loved more than you know, by a wise, benevolent Master who wants you to come to Him to receive life in full!

**This book and all my work is
in honor of my Master, JesusChrist.**

⋘⋙

CREDITS

In addition to the team of editors at Splendor Publishing, the editing assistance of Mike Tyler and Pastor Cris Uren have been crucial to the final version of this book, and I am deeply grateful. The tireless patience and encouragement of my wife, Dawn, has been an indispensable part of its development. Thank you, honey. The support and belief of Gerrick Gann and Mike Bolynn have been such important elements of this book's construction, that without these friends, this work would not exist. The practical and professional support of Margo DeGange and Steve Gutzler have been instrumental in helping me believe, and keeping me on track to complete this project. Also, there have been many of you who have continuously offered words of support and cheer that have helped me along the way. I am very thankful for the love and assistance of so many, who have believed in me and inspired me to make this book a reality.

Splendor Publishing

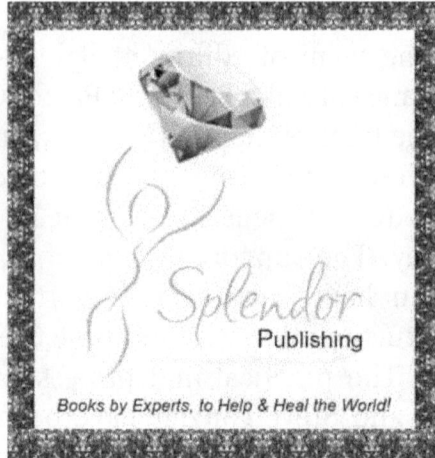

Splendor Publishing's life-changing books are written by skilled and passionate leaders, entrepreneurs, and experts with a mission to make a positive impact in the lives of others.

Splendor books inspire and encourage personal, professional, and spiritual growth. For information about our book titles, authors, or publishing process, or for wholesale ordering for conferences, seminars, events, or training, visit SplendorPublishing.com.

www.ingramcontent.com/pod-product-compliance
Lightning Source LLC
Chambersburg PA
CBHW052044090426
42739CB00010B/2036